Estate Wealth Planning Blueprint

The Ultimate Guide to Securing Your Wealth, Protecting Your Family, Reducing Taxes, Minimizing Expenses, and Ensuring Your Legacy with Step-by-Step Instructions.

Weston T. Beckett

Copyright ©2024

[Weston T. Beckett]

All rights reserved. No part of this publication may be reproduced, stored in a retrieval system, or transmitted in any form or by any means, electronic, mechanical, photocopying, recording, or otherwise, without the written permission of the publisher. Exceptions are made for reviewers who may quote brief passages in a review published in a newspaper, magazine, or website.

Publisher: [Weston T. Beckett]

Edition: 2024

TABLE OF CONTENTS

INTRODUCTION 5
CHAPTER 1 7
Introduction to Estate Planning 7
   Definition and Goals of Estate Planning 7
   Benefits of Having an Estate Plan 9
   Common Misconceptions About Estate Planning 10
   Key Terms and Concepts 11
   Life Stages and Estate Planning 12

CHAPTER 2 15
The Role of Wills in Estate Planning 15
   Differences between Wills and Living Trusts 15
   Elements of a Valid Will 17
      Competence and Capacity 17
      Written Form 17
      Witnesses and Signatures 18
      Clear Instructions 18
   Common Pitfalls in Drafting Wills 19
   Periodic Review and Updates 20
   Key Considerations for Choosing Between Wills and Living Trusts 22

CHAPTER 3 24
Setting Up Living Trusts 24
   Types of Living Trusts 25
   Steps to Create a Living Trust 26
   Revocable vs. Irrevocable Trusts 26
   Funding Your Living Trust 28
   Choosing Between Living Trust Types 29

CHAPTER 4 32
Protecting Your Assets 32
   Understanding Asset Protection 33
   Use of Irrevocable Trusts 34
   Asset Protection Trusts (APTs) 35
   Role of LLCs and Corporations 36
   Key Takeaways and Practical Tips 38

CHAPTER 5
Minimizing Taxes
- *Tax Implications of Estate Planning* 41
- *Utilizing Lifetime Gifts* 43
- *Charitable Giving Benefits* 45
- *Generation-Skipping Transfer Tax* 46
- *Utilizing Trusts for Tax Efficiency* 48

CHAPTER 6
Planning for Incapacity
- *Durable Power of Attorney* 50
- *Healthcare Directives* 51
- *Guardianships and Conservatorships* 53
- *Living Wills* 54
- *Choosing the Right Agent* 55

CHAPTER 7
Special Considerations for Minor Beneficiaries
- *Custodianship Accounts* 57
- *Benefits of Custodianships* 59
- *Setting Up Custodianship Accounts* 60
- *Limits and Considerations* 62
- *Choosing a Guardian* 63

CHAPTER 8
Estate Planning for Special Needs Beneficiaries
- *Special Needs Trusts* 66
- *Government Benefit Considerations* 68
- *Trustee Selection* 69
- *Letter of Intent* 70
- *Ensuring Financial Security and Quality of Life* 71

CHAPTER 9
Business Succession Planning
- *Valuing Your Business* 74
- *Succession Options* 76
- *Buy-Sell Agreements* 77
- *Leadership Continuity Plans* 79
- *Key Legal and Financial Considerations* 80

CHAPTER 10
Digital Asset Management
- *Identifying Digital Assets* 82
- *Access and Control Issues* 84
- *Digital Asset Policies* 85
- *Incorporating into Wills and Trusts* 87
- *Updating Your Digital Asset List* 88

CHAPTER 11
International Estate Planning
- *Cross-border Legal Considerations* 91
- *Tax Treaties* 93
- *Foreign Trusts* 95
  - Understanding Foreign Trust Regulations 95
  - Strategic Advantages of Foreign Trusts 95
  - Maintenance and Administration Challenges 96
  - Tax Implications of Foreign Trusts 96
- *Dealing with Different Jurisdictions* 97
- *Dispute Resolution Mechanisms* 99

CHAPTER 12
Charitable Giving Strategies
- *Planned Giving Options* 101
  - Types of Planned Gifts 102
  - Bequests in Wills 102
  - Donor-Advised Funds (DAFs) 103
  - Charitable Remainder Trusts (CRTs) 103
- *Setting Up Charitable Trusts* 104
- *Tax Advantages of Charitable Contributions* 106
- *Creating a Family Foundation* 108
- *Incorporating Philanthropy into Legacy Planning* 110

CHAPTER 13
Navigating Legislative Changes
- *Monitoring Legislative Changes* 113
- *Impact on Existing Plans* 115
- *Proactive Adjustments* 117
- *Engaging Legal Professionals* 118

Assessing Your Current Plan *119*
CHAPTER 14 .... **122**
Cost Optimization in Estate Planning **122**
Selecting Cost-Effective Planning Tools *122*
Avoiding Probate Costs *123*
Using DIY Templates Wisely *125*
Trusted Financial Advisors *126*
Utilizing Community Resources *127*
CHAPTER 15 .... **129**
Ethical and Family Considerations **129**
Communicating Your Wishes *130*
Preventing Family Disputes *131*
Fair vs. Equal Distribution *132*
Including Ethical Guidelines *133*
Forming a Fair Distribution Plan *135*
CONCLUSION **137**
BONUS SECTION **139**
Table 1: Asset Inventory 139
Table 2: Important Documents 140
Simple Will Template 141
Will Template for Parents with Minor Children 142
Ethical Will Template: Letter to My Loved Ones 143
Digital Estate Planning Template *144*
Table 1: Inventory of Digital Assets 144
Table 2: Digital Management Instructions After Death 145

INTRODUCTION

Estate planning might seem like an overwhelming process meant only for the rich or elderly, but it is an essential undertaking for everyone. Visualize a joyful family gathering that descends into discord over undisclosed assets and wishes. Such situations could unfortunately unfold without a comprehensive estate plan, leading to stress, confusion, and long-lasting emotional damage among family members.

This book highlights the critical role of estate planning in protecting your assets and loved ones' futures. Individuals from all financial backgrounds can benefit from establishing an estate plan. Such plans do more than protect your assets—they offer explicit guidance on executing your wishes, thus reducing potential family conflicts. Estate planning isn't just about wealth distribution; it focuses on maintaining peace and caring for your loved ones as you intend.

Many avoid estate planning, viewing it as a complex endeavor filled with legal terms. However, this book seeks to clear up these misconceptions and make estate planning more accessible. It's a common belief that only the wealthy need estate plans, but in truth, they are beneficial for anyone wishing to ensure their intentions are honored, regardless of their wealth or age.

Additionally, estate planning should not be seen as a one-off task. Life's various changes—such as marriage, divorce, or acquiring new assets—necessitate regular updates to your estate plan to keep it relevant and effective.

This book offers a straightforward guide to the essential elements of estate planning. It covers key tools like wills, which dictate the distribution of your assets upon your death, and living trusts, which help manage your assets during your lifetime and beyond. Powers of attorney are also crucial, as they authorize someone to make financial and healthcare decisions on your behalf if you become unable to do so.

Understanding these components prepares readers for the in-depth exploration of wills, trusts, powers of attorney, and other fundamental aspects of estate planning discussed in later chapters.

Our aim is to provide you with the necessary knowledge to make informed decisions, ensuring your wishes are well-defined and legally sound.

One of the most compelling reasons to invest time and effort into crafting a thorough estate plan is the array of benefits it offers. A well-crafted estate plan can significantly reduce taxes, ensuring that more of your hard-earned assets stay within the family. Minimizing probate costs is another significant advantage, as the probate process can be lengthy and expensive. By having a clear and comprehensive estate plan, you can streamline the distribution of your assets, saving your loved ones both time and money.

Moreover, a good estate plan provides peace of mind. Imagine knowing that your estate plan not only provides for your loved ones but also minimizes tax burdens, keeping more of your assets intact for future generations. This sense of security enables you to live fully, free from concerns about the future after you're gone. You can have peace of mind, knowing that your family will be looked after, and your wishes respected.

For those with minor children or beneficiaries with special needs, estate planning becomes even more critical. You can utilize specific strategies to ensure their long-term financial well-being and manage assets effectively. For example, establishing trusts allows you to control the distribution of your assets, ensuring that your children or special-needs beneficiaries are cared for in a way that suits their specific needs and situations.

This book is crafted to offer clear, practical advice for individuals starting to consider their estate planning. Although the details of estate law might seem daunting, we aim to simplify these complexities into actionable steps. With straightforward explanations and real-world examples, our goal is to enable you to confidently manage your estate planning.

Ultimately, estate planning is not merely a task to check off; it is an ongoing process that should adapt to changes in your life. By dedicating time to understand and implement a thorough estate plan, you are protecting your assets' future and ensuring your loved ones' welfare according to your desires. This book will guide you, equipping you with the necessary knowledge and confidence to navigate estate planning effectively. Let's begin this journey together, secure in the knowledge that your actions today will ensure a stable and harmonious future for your family.

CHAPTER 1

Introduction to Estate Planning

Estate planning involves strategically managing and distributing an individual's assets during their life and after their passing. It is crucial for ensuring that one's final wishes are honored, offering financial peace of mind to both the individual and their beneficiaries. This chapter unpacks the essential components of estate planning, highlighting its importance for individuals at any stage of life and any financial status. By having a well-structured plan, individuals can avoid familial disputes, lessen tax liabilities, and guarantee the welfare of their dependents.

In this chapter, readers will delve into the various facets that make up a robust estate plan. Key areas of focus will include understanding the objectives of estate planning, notably the distribution of assets, reducing taxes, and designating guardians for dependents. The narrative will also emphasize the necessity of periodically revising the estate plan to accommodate significant life events such as marriage, the birth of children, or entering retirement. Moreover, the chapter will dispel prevalent myths surrounding estate planning and elucidate crucial concepts and roles, like those of executors and trustees. By absorbing these insights, readers will acquire a comprehensive understanding of how to devise an effective estate plan that aligns with their personal needs and goals.

Definition and Goals of Estate Planning

Estate planning organizes the management and eventual transfer of assets during a person's life and after their death. This process, which involves setting out a detailed plan for asset management and personal affairs, can be complex due to legal and financial considerations but is essential for financial security.

At its heart, estate planning is about asset distribution. Individuals decide who receives assets like real estate, investments, and personal items, and they can name beneficiaries to ensure their wealth is distributed correctly. Without a clear plan, assets may go to unintended recipients or cause family disputes.

Minimizing taxes is another fundamental goal of estate planning. Estate taxes can reduce the inheritance significantly, but with strategic planning, using tactics like charitable giving and trusts, individuals can leverage tax laws to preserve more of their estate for their beneficiaries.

For families with minors or special needs dependents, appointing guardians is crucial. This ensures children are cared for by trusted individuals under unforeseen circumstances, offering peace of mind that dependents are looked after according to the parents' wishes.

The relevance of estate planning shifts through different life stages. For instance, young adults might initially focus on basic documents such as wills or powers of attorney. Marriage, however, heightens the need for comprehensive planning to align and protect partners' wishes and assets. Parenthood further complicates the landscape, necessitating provisions for children's care and financial support, typically through guardianships and trusts.

As one approaches retirement, estate planning takes on new dimensions, with decisions about asset distribution becoming more pressing and healthcare directives gaining importance. These plans help avoid complications and ensure wishes are respected in cases of incapacity.

Effective estate planning involves regular updates to reflect life changes like marriage, childbirth, or asset acquisition. This keeps the plan relevant and aligned with current needs and wishes.

When planning asset distribution, it's crucial to consider implications for beneficiaries, such as ensuring a special needs dependent doesn't lose government benefits. A special needs trust can provide financial support without affecting benefit eligibility.

Staying updated on tax laws is also vital as these can change, impacting estate planning strategies. Working with estate planning professionals ensures compliance with current laws while maximizing benefits.

Choosing the right executor is critical; this person will manage the estate through probate, handling responsibilities like paying debts and distributing assets. The executor should be trustworthy and capable of managing these tasks efficiently.

Lastly, preparing healthcare directives and financial powers of attorney ensures decisions can be made during incapacitation. These documents specify desired medical treatments and authorize someone to handle financial matters, respectively, safeguarding one's health and financial interests.

Benefits of Having an Estate Plan

Estate planning offers numerous benefits, highlighting its critical role in ensuring financial security and peace of mind. One of its primary advantages is the protection of personal assets from mismanagement or loss. Without a solid estate plan, assets often enter probate—a time-consuming and costly legal process where the court decides how your estate will be distributed. This can burden your surviving family members, adding financial stress to their emotional grief. An estate plan alleviates these issues by providing explicit directives for asset distribution, thus circumventing delays and additional expenses.

Moreover, an estate plan is essential for clearly conveying your wishes regarding asset distribution and the care of any dependents. This clarity is crucial if you have minor children or beneficiaries with special needs. By detailing your intentions in a will or trust, you guide those managing your estate after your death, ensuring your loved ones are supported exactly as you intended and eliminating any uncertainty regarding your desires. For example, you can appoint guardians for your children, create educational trusts, and earmark funds for their upkeep.

An estate plan also extends your control over assets beyond your lifetime through tools like trusts. These allow you to specify the timing and conditions under which your assets are distributed, such as staggering fund disbursements over time to prevent misuse and ensuring they are employed judiciously. You can also set conditions for asset access, like reaching certain age milestones or achieving specific goals, maintaining your influence on your estate's future use.

Additionally, a well-crafted estate plan significantly reduces the risk of legal disputes over your assets. Clear directives minimize the likelihood of conflicts among heirs, which can be emotionally and financially draining and diminish the estate's value. An estate plan, as a legally binding document, clearly outlines your wishes and reduces the chance of contested claims. It is wise to work with an attorney when creating your estate plan to ensure it complies with state laws and effectively minimizes dispute risks.

To maximize the benefits of estate planning, it is vital to adhere to several key guidelines. Begin by inventorying all your assets, including real estate, financial accounts, personal belongings, and business interests. This inventory forms the basis of your estate plan. Then, identify your goals, such as family provision, tax minimization, and charitable donations, which will influence your plan's structure.

Consider the specific needs of your dependents, particularly if they are minors or have special needs. Establish appropriate mechanisms like special needs trusts or education funds to cater to these needs. Appoint trustworthy individuals as executors, trustees, and guardians, and ensure they understand and are prepared to fulfill your wishes.

Regular reviews and updates to your estate plan are crucial, especially following significant life changes such as marriage, divorce, or the arrival of children. As your circumstances evolve, so should your estate plan to remain relevant and effective.

Common Misconceptions About Estate Planning

Estate planning is frequently surrounded by myths that deter many from taking essential actions to protect their assets and care for their loved ones. A common misconception is that estate planning is only necessary for the wealthy or the elderly, causing many people to postpone or completely neglect drafting an estate plan. Contrary to this belief, estate planning is vital for everyone, regardless of their age or financial status. It provides a systematic approach to asset management and guarantees that assets are distributed according to one's desires.

Another significant misunderstanding is that estate planning solely concerns post-death asset distribution. While this is a component, estate planning is much broader, encompassing financial arrangements during one's lifetime, especially in cases of incapacity. For example, a durable power of attorney enables a designated individual to manage your finances if you become incapacitated. Similarly, a healthcare proxy ensures that medical decisions are made according to your preferences when you are unable to communicate them.

Additionally, there's the myth that estate planning is a one-off endeavor. Some believe that once an estate plan is in place, it requires no further review. This perspective fails to consider the dynamic nature of life and financial situations. Estate planning should be regarded as a continuous process that adapts to changes in personal circumstances, such as marriage, divorce, the arrival of children, or the acquisition of substantial assets. Regular updates to your estate plan are crucial to ensure it accurately reflects your current wishes and complies with the latest legal standards, thereby providing more security and ensuring assets are distributed as intended.

Educating readers that everyone can benefit from an estate plan empowers a broader audience to take action. Estate planning is not exclusive to those with substantial wealth or complex investments. For families with minor children, it includes appointing guardians who will care for the children if both parents pass away. This decision alone underscores how estate planning serves practical purposes beyond mere asset distribution. Additionally, individuals with modest estates still need to ensure their belongings are passed on smoothly and in accordance with their desires.

Furthermore, special needs beneficiaries require particular considerations in estate planning. Creating a special needs trust can provide financial support without jeopardizing eligibility for government benefits. Such tailored strategies highlight how estate planning adapts to unique family circumstances, offering solutions that safeguard loved ones' well-being and financial security over the long term.

Addressing myths about estate planning can demystify the process and encourage proactive engagement. By understanding that estate planning is relevant to all adults, regardless of wealth or age, more people can appreciate its importance. Recognizing that it involves planning for both life and death, and requires periodic updates, helps dispel fears and misconceptions. With this knowledge, individuals can approach estate planning with increased confidence, knowing that it is an essential step toward protecting their assets and ensuring their family's future stability.

Key Terms and Concepts

In estate planning, grasping key terminology is crucial for anyone setting up or updating their estate plans. This section introduces some essential terms and concepts.

First, it's important to understand the difference between an "estate" and a "will." An estate includes all assets owned by an individual at their time of death, such as property, money, investments, and personal belongings. A will, however, is a legal document that specifies how these assets should be distributed after the owner's death. While the estate is the aggregate of one's possessions, the will dictates how these possessions are allocated to beneficiaries.

The concept of "beneficiary designation" is also vital. This involves naming individuals or entities that will receive assets. Beneficiaries can be persons, organizations, or other entities designated to benefit from the estate, either upon the owner's death or under specific conditions, such as reaching a certain age. Proper beneficiary designation helps ensure that assets are distributed according to the owner's wishes and can prevent potential disputes among surviving relatives.

Understanding the roles of "executor" and "trustee" is another critical aspect. An executor, appointed through a will, administers the deceased's estate. This role involves carrying out the wishes expressed in the will, settling debts, handling tax obligations, and distributing assets to the beneficiaries. The role requires strong organizational skills and a thorough understanding of legal responsibilities.

Conversely, a trustee manages a trust—a separate legal entity created to hold assets for beneficiaries. Trusts serve various purposes, such as tax minimization, asset protection from creditors, or providing for dependents. Trustees have a fiduciary duty to act in the best interests of the beneficiaries according to the trust's terms. They manage assets over time, distribute funds as stipulated, and ensure the trust complies with legal standards.

These distinct roles clarify the estate planning process. Executors and trustees are integral to efficiently managing and transferring assets in accordance with the deceased's wishes. Knowing who fulfills these roles and their responsibilities helps individuals make informed decisions when appointing executors and trustees.

Understanding the terms discussed simplifies communication with legal professionals, making it easier to ensure a comprehensive, tailored estate plan. It also demystifies the estate planning process, making it more accessible for those intimidated by its complexities.

For example, beneficiary designations extend beyond wills to include life insurance, retirement accounts, and bank accounts, allowing for simpler asset transfers and potentially bypassing probate. Distinguishing between executors and trustees highlights the nuanced responsibilities each role carries. Executors might navigate probate proceedings, while trustees manage ongoing financial provisions for beneficiaries like minor children or those with special needs.

In some estate plans, trustees and executors must collaborate, especially if both a will and a trust are involved. Their joint efforts help fully realize the deceased's intentions, whether through immediate asset distribution via the will or long-term management through the trust.

For families with minor children or special needs beneficiaries, it's particularly important to appoint reliable trustees and trustworthy executors. A competent trustee can manage a child's finances until adulthood or support a special needs beneficiary for life, while a capable executor can ensure smooth initial estate plan execution.

Educating oneself on these terms enables proactive engagement with one's estate plan, ensuring informed decisions about asset distribution and management after one's passing. This knowledge provides significant peace of mind and is fundamental to developing effective, enduring estate plans.

Life Stages and Estate Planning

Estate planning is a dynamic process that evolves through various stages of life. Recognizing and understanding these stages can prompt individuals to reassess and adjust their estate plans proactively. This proactive approach ensures that the plan remains relevant and effective in addressing changing circumstances.

In the earlier stages of adulthood, many individuals might not grasp the immediate necessity for an estate plan. However, this period is crucial for laying down the foundational elements. For instance, young adults often begin by establishing basic documents such as wills and durable powers of attorney. Even if they don't have significant assets, setting up these documents ensures that their wishes are respected in case of unforeseen events. Additionally, designating beneficiaries for retirement accounts and life insurance policies starts to form a rudimentary but important aspect of their estate plan.

Key moments like marriage significantly alter the landscape of estate planning needs. When two individuals merge their lives, their financial landscapes also intertwine. It becomes essential to update beneficiary designations and consider joint ownership of properties. Couples should also think about creating or updating their wills to ensure that their spouse is adequately protected. Furthermore, drafting a prenuptial or postnuptial agreement can help manage expectations and protect individual assets.

Parenthood introduces another pivotal shift. Parents naturally desire to secure their children's future, making it vital to establish guardianship arrangements within their wills. They may also want to set up trusts to ensure that their children's inheritance is managed responsibly until they come of age. As parents, planning for education expenses and healthcare provisions becomes a priority, which requires periodic reviews to keep the plans aligned with growing family needs.

The approach to estate planning continues to change as one approaches midlife. At this stage, individuals often focus on wealth accumulation and preservation. It's wise to consider more sophisticated tools such as living trusts to avoid probate and provide for seamless asset transfer. Updating power of attorney and healthcare directives ensures that in case of incapacitation, trusted individuals can make decisions on one's behalf. This stage is also an appropriate time to reassess life insurance coverage, ensuring that dependents remain financially secure.

Retirement signifies yet another critical juncture. With the cessation of regular income, retirees must pay close attention to how their estate plans manage and distribute their assets efficiently. Updating and reviewing beneficiaries, minimizing tax implications, and ensuring that the estate does not become overly burdensome on heirs are central focus areas. Additionally, retirees should review their long-term care options, including potential costs, to prevent depleting their estate due to medical expenses.

Adapting one's estate plan as circumstances evolve is not just beneficial—it's essential. Life is unpredictable, and major events such as divorce, remarriage, or the birth of grandchildren necessitate immediate updates to estate plans. Revisiting these plans periodically, ideally every three to five years, ensures that they reflect current wishes and legal standards.

Awareness of how and when to make these adjustments can prevent last-minute complications during critical life moments. For example, failing to update a will after a divorce can result in unintended beneficiaries inheriting assets, leading to legal disputes and familial discord. Similarly, an outdated healthcare directive might not accurately represent current medical wishes, putting undue stress on loved ones during emergencies.

Recognizing these life stages prompts readers to reevaluate their plans proactively. Estate planning isn't a static task; it demands regular attention and updates to remain effective. Each stage of life brings its own set of challenges and opportunities, making it necessary to revisit and revise plans to suit new realities. By understanding this evolution, individuals can ensure that their estate plans continue to serve their intended purpose effectively, safeguarding their legacy across generations.

It's helpful to consider real-life scenarios that illustrate the importance of evolving estate planning. Take, for instance, a couple who, upon reaching middle age, realize that their once-simple estate needs have grown complex with accumulated wealth and investments. They seek assistance to restructure their estate plan, incorporating advanced strategies like charitable trusts that not only benefit their chosen causes but also offer tax advantages. This restructuring provides them with peace of mind knowing that their philanthropic desires and financial goals are strategically aligned.

Or consider a retiree who, upon reviewing his estate plan, recognizes that he has not accounted for potential long-term medical care costs. By adjusting his estate plan to include long-term care insurance and reallocating some funds, he alleviates the risk of depleting his estate. This foresight ensures his heirs inherit the assets he has worked a lifetime to accumulate without substantial losses to medical expenses.

This chapter has delved into the essential components of estate planning, highlighting the importance of having a structured approach to managing assets and preserving one's legacy. It has underscored the need for clear directives on asset distribution, tax minimization strategies, and the appointment of guardians for dependents. By focusing on these elements, individuals can ensure their wishes are honored, potentially preventing conflicts and reducing financial burdens on their loved ones. The discussion also emphasized the significance of regularly updating estate plans to reflect life changes such as marriage, parenthood, or retirement.

In understanding the foundational aspects of estate planning, we've seen how having an effective plan can offer peace of mind and financial security. This chapter elaborated on the various stages of life that necessitate different estate planning needs, from establishing basic documents in early adulthood to addressing complex considerations in retirement. By adhering to the guidelines and strategies discussed, readers can navigate the complexities of estate planning with greater confidence, ensuring their assets are managed and distributed according to their wishes, thereby protecting their family's future.

CHAPTER 2

The Role of Wills in Estate Planning

Wills play an essential role in estate planning by outlining the distribution of assets after death. They provide a legal framework to ensure that one's wishes are respected and executed correctly, addressing who will take care of minor children and managing the estate's overall administration. This chapter will explore how wills fit into the larger picture of estate planning, highlighting their crucial function in preserving legacies and ensuring that beneficiaries receive designated inheritances.

The chapter delves into several key areas related to wills within estate planning. It begins with understanding a will's significance and the basic requirements for its validity. Common pitfalls encountered when drafting wills, and the necessity for periodic reviews to reflect life changes and new circumstances, are also covered. The chapter aims to equip readers with the knowledge needed to navigate the complexities of wills, reduce potential legal challenges, and achieve a comprehensive estate plan that aligns with their intentions.

Differences between Wills and Living Trusts

Understanding the differences between wills and living trusts is essential for making informed estate planning decisions that align with your individual needs. This section will clarify their purposes, functions, the impact of the probate process, privacy implications, and the procedures for making amendments.

Purpose and Functionality:

- **Wills**: A will is a legal document that takes effect after your death, detailing how your assets should be distributed. It specifies your beneficiaries, appoints a guardian for minor children if necessary, and nominates an executor to administer the estate according to your instructions.

- **Living Trusts**: A living trust manages your assets during your lifetime and after your death. You can be the trustee, managing assets yourself, or appoint someone else if you're incapacitated. Upon your death, the successor trustee you've designated ensures your assets are distributed as per your directives, avoiding probate.

Probate Process:

- **Wills** require probate, a legal process where a court oversees the will's validation, the payment of debts, and the distribution of the estate. Probate can be lengthy and expensive, often delaying asset distribution to beneficiaries.

- **Living Trusts** are designed to avoid probate. Because the trust legally owns the assets, they can be transferred to beneficiaries without court intervention, facilitating a quicker and less costly distribution process.

Privacy Concerns:

- **Wills** become public records once they enter probate, exposing the details of your estate and beneficiaries to public scrutiny. This can be a significant concern for those who prefer to maintain privacy regarding their financial and personal affairs.

- **Living Trusts** offer greater privacy since they do not undergo probate. The details of the trust remain private, safeguarding your estate's confidentiality and keeping family financial matters out of the public eye.

Amendment Process:

- **Wills** can be relatively easily amended through a new will or by adding a codicil, which is a supplement that outlines changes to the original will. This process is typically straightforward and does not usually require extensive legal assistance.

- **Living Trusts** can be more complicated to amend, especially if they are irrevocable. Revocable trusts allow for easier modifications, but both types might require the formal alteration of the trust document and potentially the assistance of an attorney, depending on the changes being made.

In summary, choosing between a will and a living trust depends on your personal circumstances, including how you prefer your assets to be handled during your life and after your death, your concerns about privacy, and how often you anticipate needing to update your arrangements. Each tool offers distinct advantages and considerations, and understanding these can help you decide the best way to protect your assets and fulfill your estate planning goals.

Elements of a Valid Will

Understanding the essential components required for a will to be considered valid is crucial for anyone involved in estate planning. Whether you're drafting your first will or updating an existing one, knowing these elements can help ensure that your will is legally sound and effective upon your passing. This subpoint details the critical aspects of validity: competence and capacity, the necessity of written form, the importance of witnesses and signatures, and the need for clear instructions.

Competence and Capacity

The foundation of any valid will starts with the competence and capacity of the individual drafting it. Legally, a person must be of sound mind and of legal age—typically 18 years or older—to create a valid will. Being of sound mind means the individual should understand the nature of creating a will, comprehend the extent of their assets, recognize the beneficiaries who are receiving those assets, and not be under any undue influence or duress.

For example, consider an elderly person with early-stage dementia wishing to draft a will. Even if they have lucid moments, their cognitive impairment might question their capacity. To prevent future disputes, obtaining a medical evaluation at the time of drafting can provide evidence of their ability to make such decisions. This ensures that the will reflects their true intentions and reduces the risk of contestation on grounds of incompetence.

Written Form

In most jurisdictions, wills must be documented in writing to be enforceable. This requirement exists because written documents offer clear, tangible evidence of one's wishes, which can be more precisely interpreted than oral declarations. Oral wills, while historically recognized in some cultures, generally lack the reliability and legal standing needed to be deemed valid today.

Written wills can be simple or complex, depending on one's needs and the assets involved. For instance, a handwritten (or holographic) will is acceptable in certain states as long as it's entirely in the testator's handwriting and signed by them. However, these too must meet specific criteria to avoid being declared invalid, such as clear language and witnessing.

To guide you through the process of drafting a written will, consider utilizing templates or consulting an estate planning attorney to ensure all legal standards are met. Templates can provide a structured format, but professional advice can tailor the document to specific state laws and personal circumstances.

Witnesses and Signatures

A will typically must be signed by the testator and witnessed to be valid. The role of witnesses is to affirm that the testator willingly signed the document and was of sound mind when doing so. The number of witnesses required can vary, but usually, two are sufficient. These individuals should be impartial parties—ideally, not beneficiaries in the will—to avoid potential conflicts of interest.

It's essential to comply with state-specific requirements regarding witness qualifications. For example, Jane wants her close friend, who is also a beneficiary, to be a witness. In this case, her friend's stake in the will could invalidate the witness's testimony due to perceived bias. Instead, selecting neutral parties, like neighbors or coworkers, minimizes the risk of invalidation.

When signing the will, all parties—the testator and witnesses—should be present simultaneously. This practice, known as "self-proving," helps fortify the will against disputes by documenting that everyone involved acknowledged each other's presence and actions. If executed correctly, this step can streamline the probate process, as courts readily accept the will's authenticity without additional proof.

Clear Instructions

Perhaps the most straightforward yet often overlooked aspect of a valid will is the use of clear, unambiguous language. Specificity in detailing asset distribution, naming beneficiaries, and assigning executors is vital to prevent misinterpretations or legal challenges.

For instance, if John owns multiple properties and simply states, "I leave my house to my children," ambiguity arises if he doesn't specify which property or how the ownership is divided. A better approach would be, "I leave my residence at 123 Main Street, Anytown, to my children, Sarah and Michael, to share equally." This clarity eradicates uncertainty and facilitates the executor's task of fulfilling John's wishes accurately.

Additionally, including contingency plans within the will can address unforeseen circumstances. Suppose a primary beneficiary predeceases the testator; specifying an alternate beneficiary ensures seamless asset transfer. Without such provisions, those assets might fall into intestacy, where state laws determine their distribution—contrary to the testator's intent.

Moreover, avoid using jargon or overly complex legal terms that might confuse readers. Simple, direct phrasing makes the document accessible not only to family members and executors but also to court officials who might interpret its contents during probate.

Common Pitfalls in Drafting Wills

When drafting wills, one prevalent error is the exclusion of key assets, an oversight that can lead to unintended consequences and complications for beneficiaries. To circumvent such issues, it's essential to meticulously inventory all assets.

Steps to Ensure Comprehensive Asset Documentation:

1. **Compile a Detailed Asset List**: Begin with tangible assets, such as real estate properties, vehicles, and personal effects like jewelry and artwork. Do not overlook items that might have substantial sentimental or financial value, such as family heirlooms or unique collectibles.

2. **Include Intangible Assets**: This category is often neglected but is crucial. List all bank accounts, stocks, bonds, retirement accounts (such as IRAs and 401(k)s), and life insurance policies. Also, consider any business interests or intellectual property rights you may own.

3. **Don't Forget Digital Assets**: With the increasing digitization of financial and personal lives, digital assets are becoming more critical. This category includes everything from social media accounts to digital wallets, cryptocurrency, and online businesses. Include access information, such as usernames and passwords, ensuring they are stored securely but accessibly for executors.

4. **Regular Reviews and Updates**: Life changes such as acquisitions, sales, or changes in relationships can affect your asset distribution plans. Regularly revisiting your asset inventory—at least annually or after any significant life event—helps keep your will relevant and comprehensive.

5. **Consult with Professionals**: Engaging with estate planning attorneys or financial advisors can provide clarity and ensure all assets are considered. These professionals can help identify often-missed assets and advise on legal strategies to optimize asset transfer and minimize taxes.

By taking these steps, you can create a clearer, more effective will that precisely reflects your wishes and ensures your loved ones are provided for as intended. Regular updates and professional guidance further safeguard against any oversights, helping your estate plan evolve with your circumstances.

Another critical error is failing to update the will after major life events. Life changes such as marriage, divorce, the birth of children, or the acquisition of new assets can render an existing will obsolete. For example, if you remarry and do not update your will, your new spouse might be inadvertently excluded from inheritance, causing emotional and financial strain. It's essential to monitor your life circumstances and revise your will accordingly. Setting a routine check-up—perhaps annually or bi-annually—or consulting with an estate planner whenever significant changes occur can help keep your will current and relevant.

Poorly written instructions within the will are another common issue that can lead to confusion and costly legal battles. Ambiguity or improper terminology can create misunderstandings among beneficiaries and may even invalidate parts of the will. Clear and definitive language is paramount. Instead of vague descriptions, use detailed information to specify who gets what, under what conditions, and in what manner. For example, instead of saying "I leave my jewelry to my daughter," specify which pieces of jewelry and any particular conditions involved. Consulting with legal professionals during the drafting process can ensure that the language used adheres to legal standards and minimizes the risk of misinterpretation.

Failing to account for the tax consequences can lead to significant financial losses for your heirs. Often, individuals do not fully appreciate the extent to which taxes can diminish the worth of their estate when it is passed on. The types of taxes that may impact the estate, such as estate taxes, inheritance taxes, and capital gains taxes, vary by location and estate size. Methods to reduce these tax impacts include transferring assets while still alive, establishing trusts, and utilizing tax-free accounts such as Roth IRAs. Seeking advice from a tax consultant or an estate planning professional is crucial to develop customized strategies that maximize the value received by your heirs.

Periodic Review and Updates

In estate planning, the effectiveness of a will is contingent upon its timely updates and revisions. A will that remains static can become obsolete, making regular reviews essential. Life events such as marriage, divorce, the birth of a child, or significant changes in financial status necessitate reassessment of one's will. These life-altering events can dramatically impact both the assets one possesses and their intended distribution.

For instance, if a person remarries and fails to update their will, they might unintentionally exclude their new spouse from inheritance rights or other provisions. Similarly, the birth of a child requires adjustments to accommodate the new beneficiary and potentially establish guardianships or trusts. Regular reviews help ensure that all assets are accounted for and distributed according to the current wishes of the individual, accommodating any newly acquired properties or investments.

The routine review of wills should also consider changing laws. Estate planning laws and regulations can shift over time due to legislative amendments or evolving judicial interpretations. These legal modifications may influence the validity and enforceability of existing wills. Staying informed about these changes is critical, and it is advisable to consult with legal professionals periodically to ensure that your will remains compliant with current laws. This proactive approach minimizes risks associated with outdated legal documents and ensures that the will's intentions are honored.

Communication with beneficiaries is another crucial aspect of maintaining an effective will. Transparent dialogue can prevent misunderstandings and potential disputes among heirs. Beneficiaries should be aware of the contents of the will and the rationale behind certain decisions. This communication fosters trust and clarity, mitigating conflicts that might arise during the execution process. Best practices for open dialogue include regular family meetings, sharing pertinent portions of the will, and explaining the decision-making process. By involving beneficiaries in the conversation, individuals can address concerns and make adjustments as needed to reflect the consensus and maintain familial harmony.

In today's digital age, embracing new technologies is becoming increasingly important in estate planning. Electronic wills and digital storage solutions offer novel ways to manage and secure these critical documents. E-wills can provide convenience through easier updates and accessibility but come with distinct considerations. It is essential to analyze the benefits and potential drawbacks of these digital formats. For example, while electronic wills can enhance efficiency, ensuring their legal recognition across different jurisdictions can be complex. Therefore, it is wise to seek legal counsel to navigate the intricacies of digital estate planning tools.

Regularly reviewing and updating wills involves establishing consistent check-ins, especially after significant life events. Major changes such as marriage, divorce, the birth of a child, or acquiring substantial assets should immediately prompt a review. Establishing a habit of revisiting the will every few years can help catch any necessary updates that may not be tied to a specific event but are still vital to ensuring the document's relevance.

Reviewing and updating a will goes beyond merely accounting for changes in assets. It also involves considering personal relationships. For instance, friendships and family dynamics evolve, and someone who was once a beneficiary might no longer be appropriate due to estrangement or other reasons. Conversely, new individuals might enter one's life and warrant inclusion in the will. This personalization and reflection of current relationships are fundamental to maintaining the will's pertinence.

Legal changes represent another critical reason for periodic reviews. Tax laws, in particular, can have profound impacts on the distribution of an estate. Changes in tax regulations might affect how much beneficiaries receive or require alterations to minimize tax burdens. Aside from taxes, other legislative changes can influence the legality and wording of certain provisions within a will. Consulting with an estate planning attorney can provide guidance in navigating this ever-evolving legal landscape, ensuring the will's compliance and efficacy.

Effective communication with beneficiaries involves more than just informing them of the will's contents. It requires a thoughtful approach to discussing the reasons behind particular allocations and addressing any concerns they might have. This engagement helps set expectations, reducing the likelihood of dissatisfaction or disputes during the will's execution. Open dialogue can also reveal previously unconsidered factors that might necessitate further adjustments to the will, reflecting a more comprehensive understanding of beneficiaries' needs and expectations.

The advent of technology has introduced new opportunities to enhance estate planning. Electronic wills, for example, offer a modern alternative to traditional paper documents. These e-wills can simplify the process of making updates and storing the will securely. However, the adoption of digital formats must be approached with caution. Ensuring that e-wills are legally recognized in the relevant jurisdictions is paramount. Additionally, considerations regarding cybersecurity and data privacy are essential, as digital wills must be protected against unauthorized access and potential cyber threats.

Key Considerations for Choosing Between Wills and Living Trusts

Choosing between wills and living trusts is an important aspect of estate planning, guided by various critical considerations. Being aware of these considerations can assist individuals in making choices that best suit their unique situations and requirements.

First and foremost, the lifecycle stage plays a pivotal role. Younger individuals, particularly those just starting their families or careers, may find wills to be more straightforward and less cumbersome. Wills are often simpler to create and do not require as much ongoing management. Conversely, individuals who are older or who have accumulated substantial assets may benefit from the detailed planning and flexibility that living trusts offer. Living trusts can be particularly advantageous for managing assets during periods of incapacity, which becomes more probable with age. They allow for the seamless management of finances without court intervention if an individual becomes unable to manage their affairs independently.

Cost implications also warrant careful consideration. Creating and maintaining a will is generally more cost-effective than establishing a living trust. Drafting a will usually involves fewer legal fees and administrative costs. However, it's crucial to recognize that while the initial setup of a living trust might be more expensive, it can save money in the long run by avoiding probate, which can be costly and time-consuming. For instance, probate fees vary significantly by state but can range from 3% to 8% of the estate's value. In contrast, living trusts can bypass this process entirely, ensuring faster distribution of assets to beneficiaries.

The complexity and effort involved in setting up these documents also differ notably. Wills are relatively simple to draft and can often be completed with basic legal assistance. They require fewer formalities and can be easily updated with codicils to reflect life changes. On the other hand, living trusts demand more intricate legal work upfront. The process involves transferring ownership of assets into the trust, which can be labor-intensive and requires meticulous attention to detail. Furthermore, maintaining a living trust requires continual oversight to ensure all assets are correctly titled in the name of the trust, thus adding another layer of complexity.

Flexibility needs are another critical aspect to consider. Wills are static documents that come into effect only after death, dictating how assets should be distributed posthumously. However, they lack the versatility that some individuals may require during their lifetime, especially in managing unforeseen changes such as financial shifts, health issues, or family dynamics. Living trusts offer greater flexibility and control over one's assets while still alive. They facilitate the management of assets in case of incapacitation and allow for modifications as circumstances evolve. For instance, if an individual plans to acquire new property or make substantial investments, a living trust can be readily adjusted to incorporate these assets without the need for extensive legal revisions.

It is also important to highlight the influence of personal circumstances on these decisions. Families with minor children or special needs beneficiaries must prioritize strategies that ensure long-term financial security and asset management. A trust can provide structured, controlled distributions that cater to the specific requirements of such dependents. This level of customization can safeguard against potential mismanagement of assets and ensure sustained support over time.

In this chapter, we have examined the integral role of wills in the broader context of estate planning. We discussed their significance in asset distribution, outlined essential components for validity, and highlighted common pitfalls that can undermine their effectiveness. The necessity of periodic reviews was stressed to ensure that wills remain relevant amidst life's inevitable changes. Understanding these elements helps demystify the process, making it more approachable for individuals contemplating or revisiting their estate plans.

By grasping the nuances of drafting and maintaining a valid will, readers can better protect their assets and ensure their intentions are honored. This chapter empowers you with knowledge about the importance of careful planning, the benefits of regular updates, and the critical nature of precise language. As you proceed with your estate planning journey, remember that an informed approach can safeguard your legacy and provide peace of mind for you and your loved ones.

CHAPTER 3

Setting Up Living Trusts

Creating living trusts is a key element of estate planning, designed to ensure that your assets are handled and distributed according to your intentions. Living trusts provide an efficient alternative to the often time-consuming and costly probate process, offering a more seamless method for transferring property and assets to beneficiaries. Moreover, they maintain privacy, as the trust's details remain confidential, unlike wills, which become public record. Whether your goal is asset protection, tax management, or providing for loved ones with special needs, it is essential to understand the process of setting up and managing a living trust.

In this chapter, we will explore the different types of living trusts and their benefits. You'll discover Revocable Living Trusts, which offer flexibility throughout your lifetime, and Irrevocable Living Trusts, known for their robust asset protection and tax advantages. We will also discuss Testamentary Trusts, ideal for managing assets on behalf of minor children or dependents, and Special Needs Trusts, which ensure that beneficiaries with disabilities can receive extra support without jeopardizing their government assistance. Additionally, we will outline the steps involved in establishing a living trust, including identifying your objectives, selecting a trustee, preparing the trust document, and properly funding the trust. This chapter provides a thorough guide to help you make well-informed decisions when creating a living trust tailored to your specific needs and goals.

Types of Living Trusts

When planning your estate, it's essential to understand the various types of living trusts, as each is designed to address different needs and scenarios. This section will delineate the primary forms of living trusts: Revocable Living Trusts, Irrevocable Living Trusts, Testamentary Trusts, and Special Needs Trusts.

A Revocable Living Trust provides control and adaptability during the grantor's lifetime, allowing modifications or revocation as circumstances change. This flexibility is advantageous for those who might acquire new assets or undergo changes in family dynamics, such as marriage or divorce. Additionally, it streamlines the transfer of assets upon the grantor's death by bypassing probate, facilitating a quicker and less cumbersome distribution to beneficiaries.

In contrast, an Irrevocable Living Trust is set and generally cannot be changed once established. This permanence offers significant asset protection against creditors and legal judgments by removing the assets from the grantor's personal estate. It also provides potential tax advantages, particularly in reducing estate taxes, making it beneficial for those with larger estates.

Testamentary Trusts are created within a will and activated upon the grantor's death, making them ideal for managing and allocating assets for minors or dependents. These trusts ensure that assets are managed and distributed according to the grantor's specifications, providing structured support over time.

Special Needs Trusts are tailored for beneficiaries with disabilities, helping preserve their eligibility for critical government programs like Supplemental Security Income (SSI) and Medicaid. These trusts allow for financial support without compromising access to government aid, ensuring beneficiaries receive necessary care alongside public assistance.

Selecting the appropriate living trust depends on personal needs and goals, from the adaptability of a Revocable Living Trust to the protective measures of an Irrevocable Living Trust, the structured care of a Testamentary Trust, or the specialized support of a Special Needs Trust.

Consulting with an estate planning attorney is crucial to effectively navigate these options. A skilled lawyer can offer tailored advice and assist in drafting documents that reflect your estate planning intentions, ensuring your assets are managed according to your wishes and continue to benefit your heirs after your departure. This professional guidance transforms complex estate planning concepts into practical strategies that safeguard your family's financial future.

Steps to Create a Living Trust

Establishing a living trust is a fundamental component of effective estate planning, ensuring your assets are managed and distributed according to your specific wishes. Simplifying this process into clear steps can make it more accessible.

Firstly, identify your objectives for the trust. Consider what you hope to accomplish by establishing the trust. Are you aiming to protect assets for your beneficiaries, bypass the probate process, or take advantage of potential tax benefits? For those with minor children or beneficiaries with special needs, the primary goal may be ensuring long-term financial security. Defining these goals upfront will help tailor the trust to your needs.

Next, select a trustee who will oversee the management of the trust, including making decisions about asset distribution and investment. Choose someone reliable with the requisite financial expertise. This could be a trusted family member, a friend, or a professional fiduciary such as a bank or trust company, which might offer greater expertise and impartiality, albeit at a higher cost. Also, appoint a successor trustee to take over if the original trustee is unable to fulfill their duties, thus maintaining continuity.

The subsequent step involves drafting the trust document with precise details on asset management and distribution. This document will outline the trustee's powers and responsibilities, the rights of the beneficiaries, and any specific asset management instructions you have. Due to the legal complexities, it is advisable to work with an attorney who specializes in estate planning. This ensures that the trust aligns with state laws and accurately reflects your intentions.

Finally, the trust document needs to be properly executed by signing and notarizing it to make it legally binding. This usually requires signing in the presence of witnesses and a notary public, following your state's specific legal requirements for such documents. This formalization step is crucial in establishing the trust's validity and enforceability.

By approaching the process step by step, setting up a living trust becomes a structured and manageable task, ensuring your assets are protected and distributed as you intend.

Revocable vs. Irrevocable Trusts

Revocable and irrevocable trusts serve distinct purposes in estate planning, each offering unique benefits suited to different scenarios. Understanding these differences is vital for selecting the right type of trust for your needs and objectives.

Flexibility and Control Revocable trusts are highly flexible, allowing the grantor to alter or dissolve the trust as needed throughout their lifetime. This adaptability is ideal for individuals whose financial situations or family circumstances are prone to change, such as acquiring new assets or experiencing life events like marriage or the birth of a child. The ability to adjust the trust without facing legal barriers provides a convenient way to keep estate plans current and aligned with the grantor's intentions.

In contrast, irrevocable trusts are much less flexible. Once established, their terms cannot be changed without the consent of the beneficiaries or a court order. The fixed nature of irrevocable trusts might seem restrictive, but it offers a layer of certainty and commitment to the laid-out plan, which can be comforting for those who desire to secure their arrangements permanently.

Asset Protection Irrevocable trusts excel in asset protection. By transferring ownership of assets into the trust, they are shielded from the grantor's creditors and legal challenges, preserving them for future beneficiaries. This is particularly useful for long-term planning like Medicaid eligibility or safeguarding against potential lawsuits.

On the other hand, revocable trusts offer no such protection during the grantor's lifetime; the assets remain accessible to creditors since the grantor retains control over them. While revocable trusts are effective for directing asset distribution after death, they do not protect those assets while the grantor is alive.

Tax Implications Irrevocable trusts can provide significant tax benefits, especially concerning estate taxes. By removing assets from the grantor's taxable estate, these trusts can greatly reduce the estate tax burden on the heirs. Some irrevocable trusts also offer income tax benefits, like charitable remainder trusts, which can enable the grantor to receive tax deductions for charitable contributions.

Revocable trusts, however, do not afford such tax advantages. Assets in a revocable trust are still counted within the grantor's estate for tax purposes, meaning they do not alleviate estate tax liabilities. Nevertheless, they simplify the asset transfer post-death, potentially reducing administrative costs and avoiding the probate process.

Administrative Complexity Revocable trusts are generally simpler and less cumbersome to manage due to their flexible nature. The grantor maintains control over the trust assets, making it easier to manage without significant legal or administrative burdens.

Conversely, irrevocable trusts involve more complex administration due to their permanent and rigid setup, often requiring the ongoing involvement of legal and financial advisors to ensure compliance with various regulatory requirements and to maintain the trust's effectiveness.

Choosing between a revocable and irrevocable trust depends on your specific needs for flexibility, asset protection, tax planning, and willingness to manage administrative complexities. It's essential to consult with an estate planning professional to navigate these choices and develop a trust structure that best aligns with your personal goals and family circumstances. This professional guidance is key to making informed decisions and implementing a trust that effectively supports your estate planning strategy.

Funding Your Living Trust

Properly funding a living trust is essential for its effectiveness and efficiency in managing and distributing your assets according to your wishes. Understanding how to correctly transfer assets into the trust is crucial for avoiding probate, maintaining privacy, and ensuring assets are managed as intended.

Basics of Funding a Trust Funding a trust requires transferring ownership of assets from your name to that of the trust. This step ensures that the assets fall under the trust's control and are not subject to probate, thus avoiding potential legal issues that may arise from improperly titled assets. For example, if a property isn't transferred to the trust, it may still go through probate, undermining the primary benefit of the trust. A well-funded trust allows the trustee to manage assets directly, enhancing asset protection and management.

Transferring Different Asset Types Assets must be re-titled to reflect the trust as the new owner, which involves specific processes depending on the asset type:

- **Real Estate:** This typically requires drafting and recording a new deed with the trust named as the owner. Legal professionals should oversee this process to ensure compliance with state laws and the accuracy of the transfer.

- **Bank and Financial Accounts:** Transferring these accounts into a trust generally involves providing the financial institution with a copy of the trust document and having the accounts re-titled in the trust's name. Each institution may have unique requirements or forms to complete the transfer.

Ongoing Management and Reviews Regularly reviewing the trust's holdings is vital, especially as you acquire new assets. This ensures all new assets are incorporated into the trust and receive the same protections. Conducting annual or biannual reviews with the help of a financial advisor or attorney can keep the trust up-to-date and comprehensive.

Addressing Liabilities When transferring assets like real estate that may have associated debts or mortgages, it's important to manage how these liabilities are handled within the trust to prevent disputes and ensure financial clarity.

Record Keeping Maintaining detailed records of all transfers into the trust is crucial for transparency and accountability. These records are valuable in resolving potential disputes among beneficiaries by showing compliance with the trust's terms and the grantor's intentions.

Communication with Beneficiaries Informing beneficiaries about the trust and its basic terms can set clear expectations and facilitate smoother transitions, reducing the likelihood of conflicts.

Incorporating New Acquisitions Develop a strategy for automatically including newly acquired assets into the trust, such as designating the trust as the default owner for new purchases. This approach helps ensure continuous protection and adherence to the trust's stipulations.

Regular Updates to the Trust Document Stay abreast of changes in laws, tax regulations, or personal circumstances that might necessitate updates to the trust agreement. Regular consultations with estate planning professionals can help keep the trust current and effective.

Compliance with State Laws Given that trust laws can vary significantly by jurisdiction, understanding and adhering to the specific regulations of your state is essential. Legal guidance is invaluable for navigating these complexities and ensuring the trust meets all legal requirements.

By following these guidelines, you can ensure your living trust is fully funded and effectively managed, providing peace of mind and securing your legacy according to your exact wishes.

Choosing Between Living Trust Types

To make informed decisions about trust choices, it's essential first to evaluate your specific needs and those of your family. Establishing a living trust isn't a one-size-fits-all solution; it requires careful consideration of various personal factors. Start by reflecting on your financial situation, long-term goals, and the unique needs of your beneficiaries. For example, if you have substantial assets and are concerned about probate costs, a living trust can help streamline the transition process for your heirs. Similarly, family dynamics, such as having dependents or relatives with special needs, may significantly influence the type of trust that's most appropriate for your circumstances.

Assessing personal and family needs involves both an understanding of current assets and future planning. Are there minor children who will need financial support in the years to come? Are there elderly parents or siblings with disabilities who require lifelong care? It's important to consider these aspects because each scenario might demand different kinds of trusts. The goal is to ensure that the distribution and management of your assets align with your wishes and adequately cover your beneficiaries' needs without causing unnecessary financial strain or legal complications.

One critical aspect to consider when evaluating needs is the presence of minor children or any other dependents who cannot manage their assets independently. Testamentary trusts come into play here. These trusts are established within a will and only take effect upon the grantor's death. They help ensure that minor children or dependents receive their inheritance in a managed manner, which can include educational expenses, healthcare, and general welfare. By setting up a testamentary trust, you ensure that the assets earmarked for minors are safeguarded against misuse until they reach an age where they can responsibly handle their inheritance.

A practical example would be parents who want to ensure their minor children can attend college. Setting up a testamentary trust allows them to specify that funds should be used for educational purposes, providing peace of mind that the children's future is secure, even if the parents pass away prematurely. This foresight is vital for families with young children, ensuring that guardianship and financial matters are clearly delineated, reducing potential conflicts among surviving family members.

Selecting an appropriate trust often involves establishing special needs trusts, which are crafted to safeguard the financial interests of beneficiaries with disabilities without affecting their qualification for public assistance programs like Supplemental Security Income (SSI) or Medicaid. These trusts offer supplementary funds for discretionary expenses that are not addressed by governmental support, such as advanced therapeutic sessions, leisure pursuits, or items for personal care. The primary benefit of these trusts is enhancing the beneficiary's quality of life while preserving their access to vital services.

Creating a special needs trust requires detailed planning, often involving legal and financial advisors to ensure compliance with regulatory standards and to maximize the available resources for the beneficiary. For instance, a parent of a child with autism might set up a special needs trust to cover specialized education, therapy sessions, and other individual-specific requirements that state programs do not adequately fund. This ensures that the child continues to receive comprehensive care throughout their lifetime, adhering to both legal and familial expectations.

Finally, when considering different trust types, it's paramount to think about future flexibility. Life circumstances can change, sometimes unexpectedly, making it necessary to revisit and possibly revise estate plans. Revocable trusts offer significant flexibility since they can be altered or revoked by the grantor during their lifetime. This adaptability means you can adjust the terms of the trust if your financial situation changes, if you acquire new assets, or if your family structure changes due to events like marriage or divorce.

For instance, suppose you're a middle-aged professional who sets up a revocable trust early in your career. As you advance professionally and build more wealth, or perhaps as you marry and start a family, you can modify the trust to reflect these changes. This kind of trust allows you to retain control over your assets while you are alive and mentally capable, providing a safety net that evolves alongside your life circumstances.

In this chapter, we have explored the various types of living trusts and their distinct advantages. From the flexibility of Revocable Living Trusts to the robust asset protection and tax benefits of Irrevocable Living Trusts, each type serves specific needs. Testamentary Trusts and Special Needs Trusts provide tailored solutions for managing assets designated for minors or beneficiaries with disabilities. Choosing the right trust depends on individual circumstances, goals, and family dynamics.

Proper estate planning involves understanding the options and making informed decisions that align with your long-term objectives. Consulting with an estate planning attorney can help ensure your living trust is set up correctly and functions according to your wishes. With careful planning and professional guidance, you can secure your family's financial future and simplify the management and transfer of your assets. This thoughtful approach provides peace of mind, knowing that your loved ones will be cared for following your intentions.

CHAPTER 4

Protecting Your Assets

Protecting your assets involves implementing strategies to shield your wealth from various legal and financial threats. Much like one would secure a valuable heirloom or insure significant properties, safeguarding your finances ensures that the fruits of your hard work are protected and accessible for future generations. Asset protection is a fundamental aspect of comprehensive estate and financial planning, encompassing a range of techniques designed to minimize risk and preserve wealth.

In this chapter, we will explore the importance of asset protection by comparing it to familiar forms of insurance. We will delve into common threats such as lawsuits, creditor claims, divorce, and bankruptcy, illustrating how these risks can impact your financial stability. The discussion will further cover robust protective measures like utilizing trusts, diversifying investments, and choosing appropriate legal instruments tailored to your unique circumstances. Furthermore, we will touch upon the integration of insurance into your protection plan and the relevance of regularly updating your strategies in light of evolving laws and personal situations. By the end, you'll have a clear understanding of how to effectively secure your assets for yourself and your loved ones.

Understanding Asset Protection

Asset protection is a critical component of estate planning, designed to safeguard your wealth from potential legal and financial threats. The ultimate goal of this subpoint is to demystify asset protection strategies and illustrate their importance in an effective estate plan.

The first point to consider is the importance of asset protection. Just as you would insure your home or car against potential loss, protecting your assets shields them from various risks. This protection ensures that your wealth remains secure for your family's future. Whether through lawsuits, creditor claims, or other unforeseen circumstances, financial losses can occur suddenly and unexpectedly. By implementing robust asset protection strategies, you not only mitigate these risks but also enhance the overall security of your family's financial future. This peace of mind allows you to focus on building and enjoying your wealth without constantly worrying about potential threats.

Next, understanding the common threats to your assets is vital. Litigation, often unpredictable and costly, presents a significant risk. A single lawsuit can drain substantial resources, especially if it involves contentious issues like personal injury claims or business disputes. Divorce, another prevalent threat, typically involves the division of assets, which can drastically alter your financial standing. Creditor claims arise when debts are pursued by individuals or entities you owe money to. Bankruptcy is a threat often faced by those with unmanageable debt levels, leading to potential seizure of assets. Identifying these threats early allows for proactive defense strategies that can protect your wealth long before any issues arise.

The cornerstone of effective asset protection lies in a few fundamental practices. Firstly, allocating assets into safer investment vehicles helps in reducing exposure to risks. For example, placing assets in trusts can provide a barrier against direct claims by potential litigants. Another critical tactic is asset diversification. By spreading your investments across different asset types like real estate, equities, and bonds, you mitigate the risks associated with market volatility. This approach ensures that a slump in one area doesn't compromise your entire portfolio. Legal instruments are key to implementing these strategies, with tools such as irrevocable trusts, family limited partnerships, and charitable foundations playing integral roles in a well-rounded asset protection plan.

Choosing appropriate strategies requires customization to fit personal situations. Effective asset protection varies greatly among individuals, influenced by unique financial conditions, family structures, and long-term objectives. It's vital to find a balance between securing assets and retaining control over them. Some methods, like placing assets into an irrevocable trust, provide robust protection but may restrict your ability to alter the trust terms later. It's crucial to understand the trade-offs associated with different asset protection strategies, often necessitating the advice of legal and financial experts to develop a plan that offers both security and flexibility.

A holistic approach to selecting asset protection strategies involves assessing your existing asset configuration and pinpointing areas at risk. Business owners, for example, should evaluate their company's structure, considering options like forming a Limited Liability Company (LLC) or incorporating to separate personal assets from business debts, thereby adding a protective layer. Homeowners should investigate state-specific homestead exemptions that protect the main residence from certain creditor claims. Additionally, retirement accounts, such as IRAs and 401(k)s, are often shielded by federal law, representing essential elements of an asset protection strategy.

Another element to consider is the integration of insurance into your asset protection plan. While insurance alone cannot provide complete protection, it serves as a critical first line of defense. Adequate liability coverage, umbrella policies, and specialized insurance products can cover significant portions of potential losses. For instance, in the event of a lawsuit resulting from a car accident, a robust auto insurance policy supplemented by an umbrella policy could prevent the victim from targeting your personal assets for compensation.

It's also important to stay informed about changes in laws and regulations that could impact your asset protection strategy. Laws governing asset protection can vary significantly by state and may change over time. Regular reviews of your estate plan ensure that it stays current and continues to offer optimal protection. This adaptability is crucial, particularly in light of evolving personal circumstances such as marriage, divorce, the birth of a child, or significant changes in financial status.

Families with minor children or special needs beneficiaries need specific strategies for long-term financial security and asset management. Setting up special needs trusts can ensure that beneficiaries receive the care and support they need without affecting their eligibility for public benefits. Similarly, educational trusts can secure funds for future educational expenses, providing peace of mind that these important aspects are taken care of.

Use of Irrevocable Trusts

An irrevocable trust is a powerful mechanism for asset protection, designed to safeguard your resources against legal and financial challenges. Once set up, an irrevocable trust is fixed—it cannot be modified or rescinded. This immutability is a key attribute that sets it apart from other trust forms, offering a shield against creditors and legal actions. This level of protection is especially valuable for those concerned about possible future claims on their assets.

The tax advantages of irrevocable trusts add to their utility in asset protection. By transferring assets into such a trust, you can potentially benefit from reduced tax rates on the income those assets generate. Treated as an independent taxable entity, the trust may receive more advantageous tax handling. Moreover, irrevocable trusts can contribute to estate tax savings, enhancing your overall tax planning and possibly diminishing the tax liabilities your estate faces.

Irrevocable trusts serve well in particular circumstances, providing solutions customized to individual requirements. For instance, parents with special needs children can create these trusts to support their children financially while maintaining their eligibility for public benefits, thus securing the child's lifestyle without risking crucial support. Business owners might establish irrevocable trusts to separate their personal assets from business liabilities, protecting personal finances from business risks. Moreover, families aiming to safeguard their wealth for future generations find these trusts beneficial in preserving their financial legacy against potential legal disputes.

Asset Protection Trusts (APTs)

Asset Protection Trusts (APTs) are invaluable tools for anyone looking to safeguard wealth against potential claims while still benefiting from the assets. These trusts leverage favorable legal frameworks to provide a robust shield against creditors. By understanding APTs, you can take proactive steps to ensure your hard-earned wealth remains secure for future generations.

APTs are created specifically to offer protection against creditors' claims, allowing the trust creator to continue enjoying the benefits of the assets held within it. These trusts are established in jurisdictions with laws that favor asset protection, which means they can offer significant advantages over other types of trusts. The primary purpose of an APT is to place assets beyond the reach of potential claimants while ensuring the creator can still derive value from these assets.

One of the key benefits of APTs is their ability to provide substantial protection while still allowing income access. This makes them particularly attractive to individuals who want to maintain their standard of living without exposing their assets to risks. Furthermore, APTs enhance estate planning flexibility. They allow for customization in terms of asset distribution, making it easier to plan for various contingencies and family needs. Additionally, APTs help maintain personal privacy by shielding assets from public disclosure. Unlike some other estate planning tools, the details of assets placed in an APT typically do not become a matter of public record.

Despite these benefits, there are challenges and important considerations to keep in mind when establishing an APT. One of the primary challenges is understanding the state-specific laws governing these trusts. Each jurisdiction has its own set of rules and regulations, which can impact the effectiveness of asset protection. Therefore, it is crucial to conduct thorough research or consult with legal experts familiar with the applicable laws in your chosen jurisdiction.

Legal guidance is essential during the establishment of an APT. Given the complexities involved, hiring experienced legal counsel ensures that the trust is set up correctly and complies with all relevant legal requirements. Without expert advice, there is a risk of inadvertently creating a trust that fails to offer the intended protections.

Clear communication with beneficiaries about the trust's purpose is also vital. Since APTs involve placing assets into a trust for protection, it's important that beneficiaries understand why this step is being taken and how it impacts them. Transparent communication helps avoid misunderstandings and ensures everyone involved is on the same page regarding the trust's objectives and terms.

Establishing an APT involves several critical steps. First, selecting the right jurisdiction is paramount. Not all states offer the same level of protection, so choosing a jurisdiction known for strong asset protection laws can significantly enhance the effectiveness of your trust. Jurisdictions like Nevada, South Dakota, and Delaware are often cited as favorable options due to their robust legal frameworks.

The next crucial step involves consulting with experienced legal counsel. A qualified attorney will navigate you through the intricacies of establishing an Asset Protection Trust (APT), making sure all legal requirements are meticulously met. Additionally, they can customize the trust to align with your particular financial circumstances, objectives, and any unique family dynamics.

Evaluating asset allocation is another important consideration when crafting an APT strategy. Not all assets may be suitable for placement into an APT, and it's crucial to assess which assets will benefit most from the protective features of the trust. For example, high-value assets that are vulnerable to claims, such as real estate or significant investments, are often prioritized for inclusion in an APT. At the same time, it's important to maintain enough accessible assets to cover day-to-day expenses and immediate financial needs.

Role of LLCs and Corporations

Limited Liability Companies (LLCs) and corporations are pivotal tools for protecting your assets. These entities function as legal shields, safeguarding personal wealth against potential business-related risks. Understanding how LLCs and corporations operate can be the first step in utilizing them effectively to secure your financial future.

An LLC, or Limited Liability Company, offers a straightforward way to provide personal liability protection. Essentially, this means that if your business faces lawsuits or incurs debt, your personal assets – such as your home, car, and personal bank accounts – remain protected. On the other hand, corporations formalize operations and establish a clear separation between personal and business finances. This structure ensures that personal liabilities do not interfere with business activities, thereby offering another layer of security.

Moreover, these entities present several advantages beyond just asset protection. One significant benefit is the credibility they bestow upon businesses. Operating as a corporation or an LLC may enhance the perception of professionalism and stability among clients and investors. This credibility can be instrumental in fostering business growth and attracting investment opportunities. Many investors specifically look for properties owned by LLCs to mitigate the risks associated with direct property ownership.

Another advantage is the operational flexibility offered by LLCs. Unlike corporations, which have stringent structures and require regular board meetings and adherence to corporate formalities, LLCs offer more relaxed management requirements. This flexibility allows business owners to tailor the management structure to suit their specific needs while maintaining the necessary legal protections.

However, setting up and running an LLC or a corporation comes with its own set of challenges. One of the primary hurdles is the initial legal cost involved. Establishing these entities requires filing appropriate documents with the state, which can incur substantial fees. Additionally, there are ongoing costs related to compliance with state regulations. For instance, both LLCs and corporations must file annual reports and pay franchise taxes, depending on the state in which they operate.

Operational responsibilities also pose challenges. Running an LLC or a corporation demands diligent attention to record-keeping and separating personal and business expenses. Mixing personal and business finances can lead to 'piercing the corporate veil,' a legal concept where courts disregard the entity's separate status, exposing personal assets to business liabilities. Therefore, it is crucial to maintain meticulous records and follow formal operating procedures to preserve the entity's protective benefits.

To maximize asset protection through LLCs and corporations, adhering to best practices is essential. One effective strategy is regularly updating operating agreements. An operating agreement outlines the management and operational structure of an LLC, detailing the roles and responsibilities of members. Keeping this document current ensures that the business adapts to changes in operation and continues to meet legal requirements.

Maintaining a clear distinction between personal and business finances is equally important. Use separate bank accounts and credit cards for business transactions. Document every expense and income, linking them explicitly to the business entity. This practice helps avoid any intermingling of funds, which could jeopardize the protective barrier between personal and business assets.

Consultation with legal and financial professionals is another best practice for those utilizing LLCs and corporations for asset protection. Legal experts can provide guidance on maintaining compliance with state regulations, drafting robust operating agreements, and navigating complex legal issues. Financial advisors can help manage the financial aspects, ensuring that the entity remains profitable and financially sound while meeting all regulatory obligations.

Key Takeaways and Practical Tips

To effectively safeguard your wealth, it's crucial to outline key strategies and provide actionable advice for implementing robust asset protection measures. These steps are designed to shield your assets from legal and financial vulnerabilities, ensuring security for you and future generations.

A critical aspect is the emphasis on proactive planning. Early action in asset protection can prevent numerous issues down the line. By setting up defenses like trusts or transferring property ownership during stable times, you lessen the likelihood of asset forfeiture in periods of financial or legal turmoil. Procrastination in these matters often forces hasty decisions in adverse situations, potentially compromising the optimal security of your assets.

Another crucial aspect is comprehensive planning. It's vital to ensure your asset protection plan covers all potential threats and is tailored to your specific needs. This involves understanding the types of risks you face—ranging from lawsuits to creditor claims—and devising strategies that address each one. For instance, someone with significant business holdings might need different protections compared to someone whose assets primarily consist of real estate or investments. A comprehensive plan should also consider family dynamics, such as the presence of minor children or special needs beneficiaries who might require additional safeguards.

Professional advice plays an indispensable role in successful asset protection. Regular consultations with financial and legal advisors are crucial for staying updated and compliant with ever-changing laws and regulations. Financial advisors can help diversify your assets, reducing the risk associated with market fluctuations. Legal advisors, on the other hand, can guide you in setting up trusts, drafting wills, and navigating complex legal frameworks to fortify your assets against possible threats. Their expertise ensures that your asset protection strategies are not only effective but also legally sound.

Equally important is continuous monitoring of your asset protection strategies. Regularly reviewing and updating these strategies ensures they remain effective amid changing circumstances. Life events such as marriage, divorce, the birth of children, or the acquisition of significant assets necessitate adjustments to your asset protection plan. Additionally, changes in laws and regulations might render previous strategies obsolete or less effective, making it imperative to stay informed and proactive in revisiting your plans.

Implementing these strategies requires a structured approach. Start by listing your assets and categorizing them based on their nature and associated risks. Once you have a clear inventory, assess the vulnerabilities of each asset. Are they exposed to potential lawsuits? Could creditors easily claim them in case of financial trouble? Understanding these nuances helps in crafting customized protection measures.

For tangible assets like real estate, consider transferring ownership to trusts or limited liability companies (LLCs). Trusts can offer privacy and shield properties from public scrutiny, while LLCs can separate personal liabilities from business-related ones. This segregation provides a layer of protection that individual ownership cannot match.

Financial assets, including investments and savings, require a different approach. Diversification is key here. Spread investments across a mix of asset classes such as stocks, bonds, and real estate investment trusts (REITs) to mitigate risks associated with market volatility. Furthermore, setting up beneficiary designations and payable-on-death accounts can facilitate smoother transitions in the event of unforeseen circumstances, reducing the likelihood of legal disputes.

Insurance serves as another critical tool in asset protection. Adequate coverage for health, life, disability, and property can act as a financial buffer, preventing out-of-pocket expenses from depleting your reserves. Umbrella insurance policies, in particular, provide additional liability coverage beyond standard policies, safeguarding against substantial claims that could otherwise jeopardize your wealth.

Communication within the family is equally significant. Ensure that family members understand the purpose and structure of your asset protection strategies. Transparent communication helps in managing expectations and prevents conflicts that could arise from misunderstandings. Involving your heirs in the planning process not only educates them about financial management but also prepares them to uphold and continue the established protection measures.

To further ensure robustness, periodically stress-test your asset protection plan. Simulate various scenarios such as economic downturns, lawsuits, or significant health crises to evaluate the effectiveness of your strategies. Identifying potential weaknesses during these simulations provides an opportunity to reinforce your defenses before actual threats materialize.

Legal tools such as prenuptial and postnuptial agreements can offer additional layers of protection. These agreements clearly define asset ownership and ensure that certain properties remain protected in case of divorce. Such preemptive measures can significantly reduce the emotional and financial strain associated with marital dissolution.

In addition, consider the benefits of offshore asset protection. Establishing trusts or bank accounts in jurisdictions with favorable asset protection laws can provide an added shield against domestic legal actions. However, this strategy requires careful navigation of international regulations and should be undertaken with professional guidance to avoid unintentional legal pitfalls.

Lastly, cultivating a habit of financial prudence within the family can reinforce asset protection efforts. Encourage responsible spending, saving, and investing practices among family members. Educating them about the principles of financial security and the importance of protecting assets lays a strong foundation for sustaining wealth across generations.

Building a robust asset protection strategy is essential for safeguarding your wealth from legal and financial threats, ensuring long-term security for you and your family. This chapter has provided comprehensive guidance on the importance of proactive asset protection measures, identifying potential risks such as lawsuits, creditor claims, and bankruptcy. By implementing varied strategies like using irrevocable trusts, asset protection trusts, LLCs, and corporations, you can effectively shield your assets. Additionally, integrating insurance policies and staying informed about evolving laws further fortifies your financial defense.

Tailoring these strategies to your specific circumstances enhances their effectiveness. Consulting with legal and financial advisors ensures that your asset protection plan remains current and adaptive to changes in personal and regulatory environments. Regularly reviewing and updating the plan is imperative, especially considering life events like marriage, divorce, or acquiring new assets. With a thoughtful and proactive approach, you can create a resilient estate plan that secures your family's future and provides peace of mind.

CHAPTER 5

Minimizing Taxes

Reducing tax burdens is a fundamental component of estate planning, significantly affecting the financial legacy left to your heirs. This chapter is dedicated to offering detailed strategies and insights on how to legally lower estate, gift, and capital gains taxes, thus maximizing the wealth preserved for future generations.

The chapter begins by explaining estate taxes, highlighting the critical role of both federal and state laws in defining what constitutes a taxable estate. It then moves on to discuss strategies related to gift taxes, showcasing how strategic lifetime gifting can provide advantages for both the donor and the beneficiary. Additionally, the text covers capital gains taxes and strategies for managing assets that appreciate in value, aiming to enhance tax efficiency. Readers will also explore different trust structures, each offering unique tax benefits, from revocable and irrevocable trusts to those designed for specific purposes. Throughout the chapter, practical examples and straightforward advice are provided, equipping readers with the knowledge needed to navigate the complexities of tax minimization effectively and make well-informed decisions tailored to their financial and familial circumstances.

Tax Implications of Estate Planning

Grasping the tax implications in estate planning is essential for anyone looking to safeguard their assets for future generations. With the right knowledge and strategic approaches, it's possible to significantly lessen the impact of taxes such as estate, gift, and capital gains taxes on heirs. Here, we will outline key elements of these taxes and discuss various strategies to mitigate their effects.

Estate Tax Overview

Estate tax is levied on the transfer of assets from a deceased person to their heirs. Understanding how this tax is calculated and applied is crucial for effective estate planning. The federal estate tax has a high exemption threshold, meaning only estates that exceed this limit are taxed. However, estate taxes at the state level can vary greatly, with some states imposing taxes on much smaller estates. This potential for dual taxation underlines the importance of being well-versed in both federal and state laws.

The value of an estate for tax purposes includes the fair market value of all assets at the time of the owner's death, such as real estate, investments, business interests, and personal property. To determine the taxable estate value, permissible deductions like debts owed, funeral expenses, and charitable contributions are subtracted from this total. The resulting net value is what's subject to estate taxes, which are tiered, meaning larger estates face higher tax rates. Strategic planning, including the use of trusts and making charitable donations, can effectively reduce the size of the taxable estate, thus minimizing the estate tax burden.

Gift Tax Considerations

While estate taxes apply after death, gift taxes come into play during a person's lifetime. Gifts given away can impact the overall taxable estate value, making understanding gift tax rules fundamental to effective estate planning. The IRS allows an annual exclusion amount, which permits you to give a certain amount to any number of people each year without incurring gift taxes or affecting your lifetime exemption amount.

For instance, if the annual exclusion amount is $15,000 per recipient, a person can give up to this amount to multiple recipients yearly without triggering federal gift taxes. Making use of this exclusion can substantially reduce the size of one's taxable estate over time. Additionally, there are exemptions for gifts made to pay for another person's educational or medical expenses if the payments are made directly to the institution.

However, gifts beyond the annual exclusion amount count against the lifetime exemption limit. When planning, it's crucial to consider the long-term impact of large gifts, especially since they can deplete the available exemption, leaving less room for estate tax exemption later. Balancing the benefits of gifting with the need to retain sufficient assets for one's needs is key to a sound estate plan.

Capital Gains Taxes

Capital gains taxes come into play when appreciating assets like real estate, stocks, and mutual funds are sold. Understanding how assets appreciate and the tax obligations upon sale can provide significant tax savings. Unlike ordinary income, capital gains are generally taxed at lower rates, but the exact rate depends on how long the asset has been held. Long-term capital gains, from assets held for more than a year, are taxed at preferential rates compared to short-term gains, from assets held for less than a year.

For example, if someone purchased stock for $50,000 and sells it years later for $200,000, the capital gain is $150,000. For long-term holdings, this gain would be taxed at a rate ranging from 0% to 20%, depending on the seller's tax bracket. Proper timing of the sale can thus make a significant difference in the tax owed.

Moreover, stepped-up basis can be a considerable tax saving tool within estate planning. When a person inherits an asset, its cost basis is "stepped up" to its fair market value at the time of the original owner's death, potentially eliminating significant capital gains taxes if the heir decides to sell it shortly thereafter. This method can help defer or even eliminate sizable tax liabilities for beneficiaries.

Trust Structures and Tax Benefits

In estate planning, employing various trust arrangements can provide significant tax advantages, making these mechanisms essential for efficient asset management, distribution, and wealth protection. Trusts come in several forms, including revocable living trusts, irrevocable trusts, and special-purpose trusts, each offering unique benefits.

A revocable living trust provides the creator with control over their assets during their lifetime, with the added benefit of a streamlined process for transferring assets after their death. Although the assets within such a trust are counted within the taxable estate, the trust aids in avoiding the probate process, thereby conserving both time and resources. This type of trust remains flexible, allowing the creator to alter or cancel it as circumstances change.

Contrastingly, an irrevocable trust transfers assets out of the creator's taxable estate, affording potential substantial tax reductions. Upon moving assets into an irrevocable trust, the creator gives up ownership, and these assets are then excluded from their estate. This type of trust serves as a safeguard against creditors and can lead to significant estate tax reductions, making it ideal for enclosing assets like life insurance proceeds, which can then be transferred to heirs free of estate taxes.

Special-purpose trusts cater to specific family needs. For instance, special needs trusts are designed to support family members with disabilities without affecting their access to governmental aid. Additionally, qualified personal residence trusts (QPRTs) enable the transfer of residential property to heirs at a minimized gift tax rate, capitalizing on lower current market values to lessen future tax impacts.

Incorporating these trust structures into an estate plan requires careful consideration and professional guidance. Selecting the appropriate type depends on individual goals, financial status, and specific family needs.

Utilizing Lifetime Gifts

When contemplating estate planning, making lifetime gifts can be an effective strategy to reduce taxable estate value and foster intergenerational wealth transfer. One key aspect of this approach is understanding the annual exclusion amount. The annual gift exclusion allows individuals to give away a certain amount of money or property each year to as many people as they wish without incurring any gift tax. This exclusion amount is adjusted periodically for inflation, ensuring its relevance over time.

Using the annual exclusion effectively enables you to make significant transfers over several years while minimizing your taxable estate. For instance, if the annual exclusion amount is $15,000 (a typical figure in recent years), you could give $15,000 to each of your children annually. Over a decade, if you have three children, you could reduce your taxable estate by $450,000 simply through these annual gifts. This cumulative effect plays a crucial role in estate planning strategies.

Next, it's important to consider the benefits of gifting property versus cash. While giving cash is straightforward, transferring property can offer additional advantages. Property, such as real estate or stocks, has the potential to appreciate in value over time. By gifting property now, you not only decrease the value of your taxable estate but also enable the recipient to benefit from potential future appreciation. This means that any gains realized by the recipient upon the sale of the gifted property won't affect your estate's value, thereby avoiding capital gains tax implications on the donor's part.

Additionally, when transferring appreciated assets as gifts, the recipient inherits the asset's original cost basis, which can be beneficial from a taxation standpoint. Often, the recipient may qualify for long-term capital gains tax rates, which are generally lower than rates for ordinary income. To comply with tax laws and ensure accurate reporting, it is crucial to document the property's market value at the time of the gift thoroughly, including obtaining professional appraisals.

Understanding the tax implications of sizable gifts is equally important. The IRS offers a lifetime gift tax exemption that shields large transfers from immediate tax obligations up to a specific limit. Contributions that exceed the annual exclusion contribute to this lifetime cap. In recent years, this exemption has been significantly high, sometimes over $11 million. It's essential to meticulously record these large transfers as surpassing the exemption limit could lead to considerable tax liabilities.

For instance, gifting a property valued at $1 million today, while having previously reached your lifetime exemption cap, would mean the additional value is liable for gift tax. Evaluating such implications is crucial to avoid unintended increases in tax burdens or negative effects on your financial strategies. Consulting a tax professional can provide valuable guidance on how significant gifts might influence your comprehensive estate strategy.

Another key strategy involves using gifts to fund education or medical expenses. Payments made directly for someone's education or medical care can be excluded from gift taxes, provided specific requirements are met. For educational expenses, payments must be made directly to qualifying institutions for tuition. Similarly, medical expenses must be paid directly to the providers and cover services like treatment, diagnosis, or preventive care.

This method offers dual benefits: it reduces your taxable estate while simultaneously supporting loved ones' essential needs. For instance, paying a grandchild's college tuition directly not only fosters their academic growth but also aligns with tax-efficient estate planning. Likewise, covering a family member's significant medical bills through direct payments ensures these costs are excluded from the gift tax, providing tangible support without tax consequences.

Strategic gifting enables asset distribution without triggering additional tax burdens, making it a potent tool in minimizing estate size and fostering wealth transfer. Understanding and leveraging the lifetime gift tax exemption thresholds help in planning substantial gifts without unforeseen tax implications. Additionally, awareness of capital gains tax exemptions for primary residences and understanding the stepped-up basis concept further enrich these strategies.

Charitable Giving Benefits

Incorporating charitable donations into an estate plan can be a powerful method for reducing tax liabilities while contributing positively to society. One of the key benefits of charitable giving is the potential for tax deductions. When an individual makes a donation to a qualified charity, they may be eligible to deduct the amount of the donation from their taxable income. This reduction in taxable income can lower their overall tax burden. For instance, if someone in the 30% tax bracket donates $10,000, they could potentially reduce their taxes by $3,000. This makes charitable contributions not only an act of generosity but also a sound financial strategy.

Additionally, setting up charitable trusts can offer even greater tax benefits and long-term advantages. Two commonly used vehicles are charitable remainder trusts (CRTs) and charitable lead trusts (CLTs). With a CRT, a person transfers assets into a trust, allowing beneficiaries to receive income for a designated period, after which the remaining assets are donated to charity. This arrangement can provide immediate tax deductions and postpone capital gains taxes on appreciated assets. Conversely, a CLT involves providing a charity with fixed annual payments for a specific period, after which the remaining assets return to the donor or other beneficiaries. These trusts allow individuals to optimize their estate planning by potentially lowering estate taxes while supporting charitable organizations.

Donor-advised funds (DAFs) have gained popularity as flexible giving vehicles that offer considerable tax benefits. A DAF allows individuals to donate assets to a fund, claim an immediate tax deduction, and then recommend grants to charities over time. These funds offer flexibility because donors can support multiple charities without dealing with the administrative hassles. For instance, a family might establish a DAF, contribute appreciated stock, receive an immediate tax deduction, and gradually distribute funds to various charities based on their evolving interests. DAFs provide a streamlined approach to philanthropy, making it easier to plan charitable contributions within an estate plan.

Charitable giving also offers significant benefits for both nonprofits and personal legacy. For nonprofits, charitable donations provide essential funding, allowing them to carry out their missions effectively. These organizations can rely on consistent support from dedicated donors to implement programs and services that address critical social issues. On a personal level, incorporating charitable giving into an estate plan helps create a lasting legacy. It reflects the values and priorities of the donor, showing future generations the importance of generosity and community involvement. Moreover, it empowers donors to support causes they are passionate about, making a tangible difference in the world.

By integrating charitable giving into estate planning, individuals can achieve dual objectives: contributing to meaningful causes and reducing their tax burden. The potential tax deductions from charitable contributions directly lower taxable income, offering immediate financial relief. Additionally, setting up charitable trusts like CRTs and CLTs provides long-term strategic benefits, allowing individuals to support charities while managing their estate tax liabilities. Donor-advised funds present a versatile option for those who want to maintain control over their giving while enjoying immediate tax advantages.

Supporting charitable organizations through thoughtful giving enhances their capacity to bring about positive change. Foundations, educational institutions, hospitals, and numerous other nonprofits rely on generous donations to operate and expand their services. These contributions can help build schools, fund medical research, provide disaster relief, and support countless other initiatives. For the donor, knowing that their contributions are making a real-world impact can be deeply gratifying. It offers a sense of purpose and fulfillment, knowing that one's wealth is being used to improve lives and communities.

Furthermore, charitable giving can strengthen family bonds and instill values across generations. When families engage in charitable activities together, they share a common goal that transcends financial gain. This collaborative effort can foster stronger relationships and teach younger members the importance of generosity and civic engagement. By including children and grandchildren in the decision-making process, families can ensure that charitable giving becomes a tradition that endures over time.

From a practical standpoint, the process of identifying suitable charitable organizations and establishing appropriate giving vehicles requires careful consideration. Financial advisors, estate planners, and tax professionals can provide valuable guidance in navigating these decisions. By working with experts, individuals can develop a comprehensive estate plan that aligns with their financial goals and philanthropic aspirations. Advisors can help identify reputable charities, evaluate different types of giving vehicles, and understand the potential tax implications.

Generation-Skipping Transfer Tax

The generation-skipping transfer tax (GSTT) is an essential concept in estate planning, designed to prevent individuals from avoiding estate taxes by transferring assets directly to grandchildren or younger generations. The GSTT applies to transfers that skip a generation, thereby ensuring that taxes are not bypassed by omitting the immediate children as recipients. This tax can significantly impact estate distribution and, without proper planning, may lead to unexpected financial burdens on your heirs.

Understanding GSTT is crucial for those looking to optimize their estate planning strategies. If you intend to pass on substantial wealth to future generations, you need to be aware of how GSTT could affect your plans. The tax rate for GSTT is equal to the highest federal estate tax rate, which underscores its potential financial burden. By familiarizing yourself with the specifics of this tax, you can develop strategies to either avoid or mitigate its impact.

One effective strategy to minimize the impact of GSTT is through the use of the lifetime GSTT exemption. As of recent regulations, each individual has a GSTT exemption amount, which allows a certain value of assets to be transferred without incurring this tax. Utilizing this exemption effectively can help reduce the taxable portion of your estate that is subject to GSTT. For example, carefully planning the timing and amount of gifts or bequests to grandchildren or other young beneficiaries can ensure they fall within your exempted transfer limit.

Another strategy involves the establishment of generation-skipping trusts. These trusts allow you to place assets in a trust for the benefit of multiple generations while potentially reducing the overall GSTT liability. By setting up a trust that names your grandchildren or even great-grandchildren as beneficiaries, the assets can grow and be used for their benefit without immediate tax implications. Such trusts need careful drafting to maintain compliance with specific IRS rules, but they provide a powerful tool for preserving family wealth over generations.

When discussing the impact of GSTT on estate planning decisions, it's vital to consider how this tax might influence your overall strategy. For instance, if minimizing taxes is a primary goal, you might prioritize making direct gifts to your children, who then independently pass assets to their children, thus potentially avoiding GSTT altogether. This approach, however, requires trust and confidence in how the next generation will handle these assets.

Estate planning isn't just about minimizing taxes; it's also about achieving peace of mind knowing your assets will be used in accordance with your wishes. Therefore, it's imperative to balance tax mitigation strategies with practical considerations of asset management and family dynamics. Including clear instructions and safeguards in your estate plan can help ensure that assets are managed wisely and disputes are minimized among beneficiaries.

Maintaining compliance with GSTT regulations is another critical aspect of estate planning. The IRS has strict guidelines on what constitutes a generation-skipping transfer, and failing to comply with these regulations can result in severe penalties. Regularly reviewing and updating your estate plan in consultation with qualified professionals is necessary to stay current with changing laws and ensure ongoing compliance.

A practical tip for maintaining compliance is keeping detailed records of all transfers and understanding the reporting requirements associated with GSTT. Accurate documentation helps substantiate your intent and provides evidence of adherence to legal guidelines. Additionally, engaging estate planning attorneys who specialize in tax law can offer valuable insights and help navigate complex regulatory landscapes.

Utilizing Trusts for Tax Efficiency

Trusts play a significant role in estate planning, offering various strategies for enhancing tax efficiency. Gaining a thorough understanding of the different trust types and their potential to manage tax obligations is key for optimizing any estate plan.

Revocable Trusts: Utilizing revocable trusts to manage tax exposure.

Revocable trusts, or living trusts, provide flexibility by allowing the grantor to maintain control over assets during their lifetime. A major benefit of a revocable trust is its ability to bypass probate, which can save time and reduce costs for heirs. By placing assets in a revocable trust, the transfer process at death can be streamlined, possibly reducing estate taxes. Furthermore, the trust can be modified or dissolved at any point, making it adaptable to changing circumstances.

However, revocable trusts do not offer protection from creditors or lower income taxes, as the assets remain in the grantor's name. As a result, thoughtful planning is essential to ensure the use of a revocable trust aligns with broader estate planning goals.

Irrevocable Trusts: Leveraging irrevocable trusts for long-term tax efficiency.

In contrast to revocable trusts, irrevocable trusts cannot be easily modified or terminated after creation, making them useful for long-term tax planning. The primary advantage of an irrevocable trust is that it removes assets from the grantor's taxable estate. Once assets are placed in the trust, they are no longer considered the grantor's property, which helps to reduce the estate's value and tax liabilities.

Irrevocable trusts also provide protection from creditors and lawsuits, which can be particularly important for individuals with significant wealth or higher legal risk. Working with an estate planning professional is essential to ensure that an irrevocable trust is properly structured and complies with relevant tax laws.

Special Needs Trusts: Key tax aspects and benefits of special needs trusts.

Special needs trusts are created to support individuals with disabilities while maintaining their eligibility for government benefits such as Supplemental Security Income (SSI) or Medicaid. These trusts provide families with peace of mind, ensuring that their loved ones' needs are met over the long term.

Special needs trusts also offer favorable tax treatment. While the trust may generate income, it must be used to enhance the beneficiary's quality of life, rather than replacing public assistance. Contributions to these trusts can often be made without incurring gift taxes if they fall within exclusion limits, and the trust assets are protected from being considered in means-tested program thresholds, safeguarding eligibility for essential services.

Qualified Personal Residence Trusts (QPRTs): Lowering the taxable estate by transferring home ownership.

A Qualified Personal Residence Trust (QPRT) allows the grantor to transfer ownership of a home to beneficiaries while retaining the right to live in it for a set number of years. During this period, the grantor can continue to occupy the home without paying rent. Once the trust term ends, the property is transferred to the beneficiaries, and its value is removed from the taxable estate.

QPRTs provide tax benefits by reducing the estate's taxable value, as the home's market value is locked in at the time of transfer, potentially avoiding taxes on future appreciation. Additionally, QPRTs can take advantage of gift tax exemptions, allowing for a more strategic reduction of taxable gifts.

Choosing the appropriate trust term is critical when setting up a QPRT. A longer term results in a greater retained interest and a lower initial gift tax valuation, but if the grantor does not outlive the trust term, the property's full value may be included in the taxable estate. Professional advice is crucial in balancing these factors.

In conclusion, the various types of trusts discussed offer specific benefits to meet diverse estate planning objectives. Revocable trusts offer flexibility and probate avoidance, while irrevocable trusts deliver long-term tax savings and asset protection. Special needs trusts ensure continued care for beneficiaries with disabilities without compromising access to government benefits, and QPRTs allow for tax-efficient home ownership transfers.

Navigating the complexities of estate, gift, and capital gains taxes can be challenging, but employing these strategies can lead to significant tax savings and a more efficient estate plan. By making use of trust structures, lifetime gifting, and charitable contributions, individuals can optimize the distribution of their assets and secure the financial future of their beneficiaries.

Proper tax planning in estate management is key to safeguarding wealth and ensuring your estate is passed on in accordance with your wishes. Whether you are starting from scratch or refining an existing plan, these strategies offer practical steps for preserving assets. With the help of professional advice, you can make informed decisions that will benefit both you and your heirs for generations to come.

CHAPTER 6

Planning for Incapacity

Planning for incapacity is essential for ensuring your financial affairs are managed effectively if you become unable to do so yourself. When individuals face periods of mental or physical incapacitation, having a structured plan in place can alleviate stress and provide clarity for both them and their loved ones. This chapter delves into the mechanisms available to ensure that your finances continue to be handled responsibly and according to your preferences during such times.

The chapter will explore the concept of a durable power of attorney (POA), emphasizing its critical role in maintaining financial stability when you're incapacitated. It will detail how a durable POA differs from a standard power of attorney and why it remains valid even if you lose the capability to make decisions. The discussion will cover how to select a trustworthy agent, the importance of customization in the POA document, and your rights to modify or revoke it as circumstances change. By the end of this chapter, you will have a comprehensive understanding of how to safeguard your financial interests and ensure seamless management through well-structured legal provisions.

Durable Power of Attorney

Planning for incapacity is a vital aspect of estate planning that ensures your financial affairs are managed effectively when you're unable to do so yourself. One crucial component of this planning process is establishing a durable power of attorney (POA). This legal document grants a designated agent, or attorney-in-fact, the authority to manage your financial matters on your behalf, even if you become incapacitated.

Understanding the significance of a durable power of attorney begins with recognizing its unique feature: it remains effective regardless of your mental or physical state. Unlike a standard power of attorney, which becomes void if the principal (the person granting the authority) becomes incapacitated, a durable POA continues to provide the necessary legal authority to your agent. This characteristic is essential because it ensures that your financial management doesn't come to a halt just when it might be needed the most.

Continuity in financial management is one of the primary benefits of a durable power of attorney. In the unfortunate event of incapacitation, there is inherently a lot of stress and confusion. Delays in accessing funds can result in bills going unpaid, investments being mismanaged, or important financial decisions being neglected. A durable POA ensures that there's no disruption in handling your finances, as your designated agent can step in immediately to take care of banking transactions, pay bills, manage investments, and handle other critical financial tasks without waiting for additional legal proceedings.

Selecting a trustworthy agent to act under your durable power of attorney is paramount. This individual will have significant control over your financial life, so it's essential to choose someone who is not only competent and responsible but also has your best interests at heart. Typically, people consider close family members or trusted friends for this role. However, it's crucial to have candid discussions with potential agents about their willingness to take on the responsibility and their understanding of your financial preferences and values. Transparency in these conversations can prevent future misunderstandings and ensure that your financial matters are managed according to your wishes.

It is also possible to tailor a durable power of attorney to fit your specific needs and preferences. You don't have to give your agent broad, unrestricted powers if you're uncomfortable with that level of authority. Instead, you can define specific powers within the POA, such as limiting the agent's ability to manage certain accounts or requiring them to consult with another individual before making significant transactions. This customization allows you to retain control over what decisions others can make on your behalf, providing an added layer of security and peace of mind.

Moreover, even after creating a durable power of attorney, you retain the right to modify or revoke it as your circumstances change. Life is unpredictable, and relationships or financial situations can evolve over time. If, for any reason, you decide that your current agent is no longer suitable, or you need to update the terms of the POA to reflect new conditions, you can make those changes. It's a good practice to periodically review your estate planning documents, including your durable power of attorney, to ensure they still align with your current wishes and circumstances.

Healthcare Directives

Ensuring that your medical decisions are handled according to your wishes if you become incapacitated is a crucial aspect of estate planning. This section highlights the importance of having healthcare directives in place, which can provide clear guidance for family members and medical professionals.

A living will is one of the most essential healthcare directives. It allows you to specify your preferences regarding medical treatment if you face a terminal illness or an irreversible condition where recovery is not possible. For example, you may want to outline whether you prefer life-sustaining treatments like mechanical ventilation or feeding tubes or if you'd rather opt for palliative care measures that focus on comfort. By providing these instructions in advance, you ensure that your wishes are respected when you're unable to communicate them yourself, thereby alleviating the emotional burden on your loved ones who might otherwise have to make these tough decisions without your input.

Another critical directive is a healthcare proxy, also known as a medical power of attorney. This document designates a trusted individual—often called an agent or proxy—to make healthcare decisions on your behalf should you become incapacitated. Selecting this person requires careful consideration since they will be responsible for making potentially life-altering decisions. It's essential to choose someone who understands your values and is willing to advocate for your preferences even under pressure from other family members or medical personnel.

Open and honest discussions about your healthcare preferences are vital. Once you've designated your proxies, take the time to sit down and articulate your wishes clearly. Utilization of straightforward language during these conversations can help prevent misunderstandings later on. You could outline different scenarios and explain your choices, ensuring your proxies comprehend the reasoning behind your decisions. Additionally, sharing these discussions with other family members can foster support and understanding, reducing potential conflicts in tense moments.

The legal requirements for healthcare directives, such as notarization or witness signatures, can vary significantly by state. Meeting these requirements is crucial, as failing to do so could render your directives invalid when they are most needed. Some states require that your documents be notarized to verify your identity and willingness to create the directive. Others might mandate that witnesses, who are not beneficiaries or related to the agent, sign the documents to attest to their authenticity. Therefore, it's important to familiarize yourself with your state's specific rules or consult with an estate planning attorney to ensure compliance.

Regular reviews and updates to your healthcare directives are equally important. Life circumstances and medical technologies can change, necessitating adjustments in your stated preferences. For example, advancements in medical treatments might influence your choices about aggressive interventions or experimental treatments. Moreover, changes in personal relationships, such as divorce or the death of a previously designated proxy, might prompt the need for new appointments. Routinely revisiting these documents ensures they continue to reflect your current wishes and remain legally valid.

In addition to creating these documents, it's wise to keep them accessible but secure. Make copies and distribute them to relevant parties, including your primary care physician, designated proxies, and close family members. Storing a copy in a digital format can also be beneficial as many hospitals now accept electronic versions. Quick access to these directives in an emergency can expedite decision-making processes and prevent unnecessary delays in your care.

Guardianships and Conservatorships

In situations where individuals find themselves unable to make informed decisions due to incapacity, establishing a legal guardianship or conservatorship may become necessary. These legal frameworks ensure that the incapacitated individual's affairs—both personal and financial—are managed appropriately, providing peace of mind for family members and loved ones.

A guardianship is a legal arrangement in which a court appoints an individual (the guardian) to make decisions on behalf of someone who is incapacitated (the ward). The scope of the guardian's authority can vary; it may encompass making medical decisions, determining living arrangements, and overseeing general welfare. For example, if an elderly person with dementia can no longer manage their daily needs, a guardian could be appointed to ensure they receive proper care and support. This role is crucial, as it ensures the incapacitated person's well-being is maintained when they cannot advocate for themselves.

Similarly, a conservatorship is a legal tool specifically designed to manage the financial affairs of an incapacitated individual. In this scenario, the court appoints a conservator to handle tasks such as paying bills, managing investments, and safeguarding assets. For instance, if an individual has suffered a severe stroke and can no longer manage their finances, a conservator can step in to prevent financial mismanagement and protect the individual's economic interests. The distinction between guardianship and conservatorship lies mainly in the nature of the responsibilities undertaken: while guardianship covers broader aspects of personal care and decision-making, conservatorship focuses solely on financial matters.

It's important to note that the process of establishing guardianships and conservatorships can be intricate and demanding. Court proceedings typically involve submitting detailed petitions, undergoing evaluations, and sometimes facing familial disputes regarding who should assume responsibility. This process can also be time-consuming and expensive, requiring legal fees, court costs, and potentially even costs associated with ongoing oversight by the court. Families must prepare for these challenges, as the emotional strain and financial burden can be significant during such periods.

Despite the complexities involved, setting up a guardianship or conservatorship can offer a structured and legally recognized means of ensuring that an incapacitated individual's needs are met. Courts generally require evidence of the individual's incapacity, such as medical reports or expert testimonies, before granting such appointments. This rigorous vetting process helps ensure that the appointed guardian or conservator is suitable and committed to acting in the ward's best interests.

Additionally, it's crucial to understand that guardianships and conservatorships are not necessarily permanent arrangements. They can be terminated if the incapacitated individual regains capacity or if there is a change in circumstances that eliminates the need for such oversight. For example, if a ward recovers from a debilitating illness and can once again manage their affairs, they—or those acting on their behalf—can petition the court to dissolve the guardianship or conservatorship. This flexibility allows for adjustments based on the evolving needs and conditions of the incapacitated individual, ensuring that their autonomy is restored as soon as it is feasible and safe to do so.

When considering whether to pursue guardianship or conservatorship, it is essential to weigh the benefits against the potential costs and burdens. Seeking advice from estate planners or elder law attorneys can provide valuable insights into alternative arrangements, such as powers of attorney or trusts, which might serve similar purposes without necessitating court intervention. However, in cases where no preemptive measures are in place, guardianships and conservatorships remain vital tools to protect and manage the interests of those who cannot do so themselves.

Ultimately, the primary goal of establishing a guardianship or conservatorship is to ensure that the incapacitated individual receives the appropriate care and management of their affairs. By understanding the processes involved and the responsibilities entailed, families can make informed decisions that align with the best interests of their loved ones.

Navigating the legal landscape of guardianships and conservatorships requires diligence and preparedness. Each case is unique, and courts take great care in reviewing applications to safeguard the rights and well-being of the ward. The involvement of impartial experts and ongoing court supervision further adds layers of protection, ensuring that the appointed guardians or conservators fulfill their duties ethically and effectively.

Living Wills

To effectively communicate your end-of-life preferences, a living will serves as a critical document within your estate planning strategy. A living will outlines your specific healthcare wishes in scenarios where you are incapacitated and unable to articulate your desires. This not only provides you with peace of mind but also relieves your loved ones from the emotional burden of making difficult medical decisions on your behalf.

Reflecting on your values, beliefs, and personal circumstances is paramount when creating a living will. Consider what types of medical treatments align with your principles and which do not. For instance, some individuals may prioritize life-preserving measures regardless of their condition, while others might prefer to forgo aggressive treatments if they have a terminal illness or are in a persistent vegetative state. By contemplating these scenarios, you can ensure that your living will accurately represents your personal stance on various medical interventions.

Requirements for valid living wills vary by state, making it essential to be informed about the legal standards in your jurisdiction. Some states may require witnessing by two unrelated individuals, notarization, or specific forms to be used for the document to be legally binding. Research your state's specific requirements to avoid any potential issues with enforceability. Consulting with a knowledgeable attorney can help you navigate these complexities and ensure that your living will meets all necessary legal criteria.

Regular updates to your living will are crucial, especially in response to significant life changes or advancements in medical technology. Life events such as marriage, divorce, the birth of a child, or the diagnosis of a serious illness can all influence your healthcare preferences. Additionally, as medical treatments evolve, so might your opinions on what constitutes acceptable care. Reviewing and revising your living will periodically ensures that it remains relevant and reflective of your current wishes.

Incorporating a living will into your estate plan does more than just document your medical preferences; it integrates your healthcare wishes seamlessly with other elements of your overall financial strategy. When combined with other estate planning tools like durable powers of attorney and healthcare proxies, a living will creates a comprehensive plan that addresses both medical and financial aspects of your future, even in times of incapacity. This holistic approach helps protect your well-being and ensures that all facets of your life are managed according to your wishes.

A critical component of drafting your living will is communicating your choices with those who will be responsible for carrying out your directives. Having candid discussions with your family members, healthcare agents, and attorneys about your end-of-life preferences fosters understanding and minimizes the risk of disputes or confusion during emotionally charged situations. This dialogue is essential in ensuring that your intentions are honored and can significantly reduce the stress on your loved ones during difficult times.

While a living will primarily focuses on healthcare decisions, its creation process offers an opportunity for introspection and a broader contemplation of your values and goals. By articulating your medical preferences, you gain clarity on what truly matters to you, which can inform other areas of your life and legacy planning. This deeper understanding enriches your overall estate plan and reinforces the alignment between your personal values and the provisions set forth in your legal documents.

Choosing the Right Agent

Selecting the most suitable agent to act on your behalf during times of incapacity is a crucial task. This decision requires careful consideration and thoughtful evaluation of several factors to ensure that your financial and personal affairs are managed effectively and in alignment with your wishes.

The first step in this process is to evaluate candidates based on their ability to handle financial affairs responsibly. This involves assessing their financial literacy, organizational skills, and track record with managing money. For example, you might consider whether the potential agent has a history of paying bills on time, maintaining good credit, or successfully managing their own assets. It's also important to consider their familiarity with legal and financial documents, as they will be tasked with handling complex paperwork and making significant financial decisions on your behalf.

Another critical aspect is discussing your values and wishes with potential agents. Open and honest communication is key to ensuring that they understand and can align with your desires. Share specific examples of how you manage your finances, your priorities, and any unique circumstances that might influence your decisions. This conversation should include your preferences for investments, spending, and any charitable contributions you wish to make. By clearly conveying your values and expectations, you help your agent make decisions that reflect your true intentions.

In some cases, it may be beneficial to appoint more than one agent to create a system of checks and balances. Having multiple agents can provide an additional layer of oversight and increase accountability. For instance, you might designate one person to handle day-to-day financial transactions while another oversees major investment decisions or periodic reviews of financial statements. This approach can help prevent misuse of authority and reduce the risk of errors, ensuring a higher level of accuracy and integrity in managing your affairs. However, it's essential to clearly define each agent's responsibilities to avoid overlaps and conflicts.

Proper documentation and communication are vital to prevent confusion and legal issues. Ensure that all agreements are recorded in writing and that each agent receives copies of relevant documents, including your financial power of attorney and any instructions you've provided. It's also advisable to inform other family members and trusted advisors about your choices to foster transparency and understanding. Regular updates and reviews of these documents will also help keep everyone informed and aware of any changes in your circumstances or wishes.

When choosing an agent, consider not only their ability to manage financial matters but also their disposition and willingness to take on this responsibility. An ideal agent should be trustworthy, dependable, and capable of making sound judgments under pressure. It's worth noting that this role can be demanding and time-consuming, so selecting someone who is both willing and able to dedicate the necessary time and effort is crucial. In some instances, a professional fiduciary or financial advisor might be a suitable option, particularly if you have complex assets or require specialized expertise.

This chapter has highlighted the importance of managing your financial affairs during periods of incapacity through a durable power of attorney. By understanding the unique benefits of this legal tool, you can ensure that your financial management continues seamlessly, even if you're unable to handle it yourself. Selecting a trustworthy agent and customizing the powers granted can provide added security and peace of mind. Regular reviews and potential modifications to the document help maintain its relevance and alignment with your evolving circumstances.

By planning for incapacity with a durable power of attorney, you offer clarity and assurance not only for yourself but also for your loved ones. This proactive step minimizes stress and confusion during challenging times, ensuring that critical financial tasks are managed effectively without unnecessary delays. Ultimately, this thoughtful preparation fosters stability and confidence, allowing you and your family to focus on other important aspects of life, knowing that your financial affairs are in capable hands.

CHAPTER 7

Special Considerations for Minor Beneficiaries

Creating provisions for minor children in estate planning is essential to ensure their welfare and financial security in the event of an untimely loss. Structuring these provisions carefully can help manage and protect assets designated for minors, providing much-needed support during their formative years. Parents or guardians must navigate various options to set up appropriate mechanisms that safeguard a child's future while also offering flexibility and ease of management.

This chapter delves into the specifics of custodianship accounts, exploring how they function under the legal frameworks provided by the Uniform Transfers to Minors Act (UTMA) and the Uniform Gifts to Minors Act (UGMA). It will guide you through the roles and responsibilities of custodians, the types of assets that can be included, and the financial and legal implications involved. By understanding the benefits and limitations of custodianship accounts, you can make informed decisions to establish secure and manageable plans for your minor beneficiaries.

Custodianship Accounts

Custodianship accounts are a crucial tool in estate planning for families with minor children. They serve as a reliable method for managing assets that are designated for minors until they reach adulthood. Understanding how these accounts function and who can serve as custodians is essential for ensuring the welfare and financial security of your children.

At their core, custodianship accounts are designed to protect and manage assets on behalf of minor beneficiaries. These accounts fall under the Uniform Transfers to Minors Act (UTMA) or the Uniform Gifts to Minors Act (UGMA). Both acts allow parents or guardians to transfer assets such as money, securities, or real estate to a custodial account. The designated custodian manages these assets until the minor reaches the age of majority, which is typically 18 or 21 years old, depending on the state laws.

Anyone who is an adult and is deemed capable by the probate court can serve as a custodian. Most often, custodians are parents, grandparents, or trusted relatives, but friend or professional fiduciaries can also be appointed. It is important to select someone who is financially responsible and trustworthy, as they will have control over the assets and are expected to act in the best interest of the child.

Custodians manage funds on behalf of minors, ensuring that the assets are used appropriately for the child's needs. This role involves making decisions regarding the use of funds for various purposes such as education, healthcare, or other necessities. For instance, if a minor needs funds for school tuition, the custodian can authorize withdrawals from the account for this purpose. Similarly, medical expenses or day-to-day living costs can be covered using the custodianship account.

These accounts offer significant benefits by providing direct financial support for education, health, or maintenance until the minor reaches the legal age of majority. This feature is particularly valuable because it ensures that funds are available when needed most, without having to navigate complicated legal processes. For example, a child might need special tutoring or medical treatment; the custodian can allocate funds swiftly to address these needs, thereby providing timely support.

In terms of educational expenses, custodianship accounts can cover costs ranging from school fees to extracurricular activities that enhance the child's learning experience. Healthcare expenses are another critical area where these accounts prove beneficial. Whether it's routine check-ups or unexpected medical emergencies, custodial funds can be readily accessed to ensure that the child receives the necessary care. Maintenance costs, such as clothing, food, or housing, are also manageable through these accounts, thus covering the basic essentials of daily living.

One of the most appealing aspects of custodianship accounts is their simplicity. They offer a straightforward method to manage assets without extensive legal complexities. Unlike other forms of trusts or estate plans that may require ongoing legal oversight or involve intricate documentation, custodianship accounts are relatively easy to set up and maintain. Once established, the custodian has a clear directive to manage the assets according to the guidelines set forth by the UTMA or UGMA statutes.

For many families, the ease of administration is a standout advantage. There is no requirement for annual tax filings specific to the trust, nor is there the need for lengthy court proceedings to access the funds. This simplicity reduces both the administrative burden and the associated costs, making custodianship accounts a pragmatic choice for many parents and guardians.

Furthermore, custodianship accounts provide peace of mind by establishing a clear framework for asset management. When setting up the account, the donor can specify how the assets should be used, which helps ensure that the funds are utilized responsibly. The custodian's fiduciary duty legally binds them to act in the best interest of the minor, adding an extra layer of protection.

The flexibility of custodianship accounts also means that a wide range of assets can be included. From cash and stocks to mutual funds and real estate, diverse types of assets can be managed within these accounts. This versatility allows parents and guardians to tailor the account to fit their financial situation and the anticipated needs of the child.

While custodianship accounts are generally straightforward to manage, it's important to stay informed about any state-specific regulations that might apply. Each state can have variations in its interpretation and implementation of the UTMA or UGMA, affecting aspects like the age of majority or allowable investments. Being aware of these details can help prevent unforeseen complications and ensure that the account operates smoothly.

Benefits of Custodianships

Custodianship accounts offer a practical and appealing solution for estate planning, particularly when considering minor beneficiaries. One of the primary reasons these accounts are so attractive is that they can help avoid the delays and costs associated with probate and court processes. When an estate goes through probate, it often incurs significant expenses and lengthy timelines, which can cause financial strain and uncertainty for the beneficiaries. Custodianship accounts, however, allow for a more streamlined approach by transferring assets directly to the minor, bypassing the need for probate entirely.

Additionally, custodianship accounts provide a clear structure for how funds should be used, ensuring responsible management. This predetermined framework outlines specific purposes for which the funds can be utilized, such as education, healthcare, or everyday living expenses. By setting these guidelines in advance, the grantor can ensure that the assets are being used in a manner that aligns with their intentions and best serves the minor's needs. This structure also prevents potential misuse or mismanagement of funds, offering peace of mind to those planning their estates.

One of the notable benefits of custodianship accounts is that they empower selected adults to make decisions regarding the minor's financial needs. The appointed custodian acts as a fiduciary, holding and managing the assets until the minor reaches the age of majority. This responsibility includes making judicious choices about expenditures and investments, tailored to the child's unique circumstances. The custodian's role is crucial in providing ongoing financial oversight and support, particularly during the formative years of the minor's life.

Clear guidelines set for fund usage promote efficient asset management, another key advantage of custodianship accounts. These guidelines typically specify permissible expenses and prioritize long-term financial goals. For example, funds might be allocated primarily toward educational pursuits, ensuring that the minor has access to quality schooling and opportunities for higher education. Such stipulations help create a balanced approach to spending, preserving the estate's value while meeting the immediate and future needs of the minor.

In practice, custodianship accounts often involve close collaboration between the custodian and other professionals, such as financial advisors and legal experts. This collaborative effort ensures that all decisions are compliant with relevant laws and align with the overall estate plan. It also provides an additional layer of oversight, further safeguarding the minor's interests and the estate's integrity.

Another important aspect to consider is the flexibility custodianship accounts offer compared to traditional trust arrangements. While trusts can be complex and rigid, custodianship accounts tend to be more straightforward, with fewer administrative burdens. This simplicity makes them an accessible option for many families, allowing them to implement effective estate planning measures without getting bogged down in legal intricacies.

The process of establishing a custodianship account involves minimal paperwork and regulatory hurdles, making it a user-friendly choice for estate planners. Families can set up these accounts relatively quickly, ensuring that assets are protected and managed without unnecessary delays. This ease of setup is particularly beneficial in situations where time is of the essence, such as following the unexpected loss of a parent or guardian.

Moreover, custodianship accounts can adapt to changing circumstances, providing a versatile tool for long-term planning. If the minor's needs evolve over time, the custodian can adjust the management of the funds accordingly. This adaptability ensures that the estate remains supportive and relevant throughout the minor's growth and development.

Setting Up Custodianship Accounts

Establishing custodianship accounts is an essential step in the process of securing financial assets for minor beneficiaries. This subpoint aims to guide you through the necessary steps and considerations to set up these accounts effectively.

Understanding the paperwork and regulations involved in setting up a custodianship account is fundamental. The required documentation typically includes a custodial agreement, which outlines the terms and conditions under which the custodian will manage the minor's assets. Financial institutions will often have specific forms that need to be completed accurately to initiate the account setup. It's crucial to familiarize yourself with these forms well in advance to avoid any delays or errors. You may also need to provide proof of the minor's identity and your legal authority to act on behalf of the child, such as a birth certificate or court order assigning guardianship.

Regulations governing custodianship accounts can vary by state, so it's important to consult local laws and possibly seek legal advice to ensure compliance. For example, under the Uniform Transfers to Minors Act (UTMA) or the Uniform Gifts to Minors Act (UGMA), different states might have unique modifications that could affect how you manage the funds. Understanding these nuances will help you navigate the regulatory landscape more effectively.

Identifying the financial institutions involved in establishing custodianship accounts is another critical step. Not all banks and credit unions offer these types of accounts, so it's essential to research and choose a reputable institution that has experience dealing with custodianship arrangements. Meeting with representatives from several financial institutions can provide you with insights into the specific requirements and services each one offers. Some institutions may offer additional benefits, such as financial planning services or educational materials on managing custodial accounts, which can be beneficial in the long run.

When selecting a financial institution, consider factors like their fee structures, the range of investment options available, and the level of customer support they provide. Institutions with a strong track record in managing custodial accounts can offer peace of mind and ensure that the minor's assets are handled with care and expertise. Additionally, look into whether the institution offers online account management tools, which can make monitoring and managing the account more convenient.

Defining the custodian's responsibilities is another key area when setting up a custodianship account. The custodian acts as a fiduciary, meaning they are legally obligated to manage the minor's assets in the best interests of the child. This involves making prudent investment choices, keeping accurate records of all transactions, and ensuring that the funds are used appropriately according to the terms outlined in the custodial agreement.

The custodian must also be prepared to manage the account until the minor reaches the age of majority, which varies by state but is typically 18 or 21 years old. During this period, the custodian should focus on preserving the asset's value while balancing the need for growth. Regular financial reviews and consultations with financial advisors can help the custodian stay on track and make informed decisions. It's also essential for the custodian to understand the tax implications associated with the account, including any potential tax benefits or liabilities, and to comply with annual reporting requirements.

Ensuring compliance with legal requirements to safeguard assets for the minor is a crucial final step. This involves staying updated on relevant laws and regulations that govern custodianship accounts. In addition to state-specific laws like UTMA and UGMA, federal laws such as the Internal Revenue Code can impact how custodianship accounts are managed, particularly regarding tax treatment of earnings within the account.

Implementing internal controls and establishing clear procedures can help in maintaining compliance and protecting the assets. For instance, periodically auditing the account and documenting all expenditures meticulously will provide a transparent record of how the funds are being utilized. Moreover, it's advisable to keep abreast of any changes in legislation that could affect the custodianship arrangement and to adjust practices accordingly.

Preparing trust documents is another layer of protection for minors' assets. These documents should outline detailed terms of distribution, the custodian's responsibilities, and eligible expenses. Clear guidelines within the trust can prevent misunderstandings and ensure that the funds are used solely for the minor's benefit. Depending on the complexity of the estate plan, working with an estate planning attorney can help draft these documents accurately and comprehensively.

Finally, ongoing education and training for the custodian can enhance their ability to manage the account effectively. Financial literacy programs, workshops, and resources offered by financial institutions or community organizations can equip custodians with the skills necessary to fulfill their duties responsibly. Encouraging custodians to stay informed about best practices in asset management and regulatory compliance can further safeguard the minor's financial future.

Limits and Considerations

When planning for the future welfare and financial security of minor beneficiaries, it's essential to recognize the potential drawbacks and considerations associated with custodianship accounts. While these accounts can provide a structured way to manage assets for minors, they come with certain limitations that should be carefully evaluated.

To begin with, custodianship accounts may have constraints on the type of assets that can be included. Not all assets are suitable for custodial management. For example, illiquid assets like real estate or closely-held business interests might not fit well within the framework of custodianship accounts. This limitation can restrict the flexibility parents or guardians have in managing a diversified portfolio of assets for their children. To ensure the effective use of custodianship accounts, it is important to understand these restrictions upfront and plan accordingly.

Another critical consideration is the tax implications for custodians. Custodian-held assets may incur taxes, which could affect the overall financial efficiency of the arrangement. For instance, the income generated from investments held within the account is often taxed at the child's rate, which is generally lower than the custodian's. However, once the income exceeds a certain threshold, it might be subjected to higher tax rates due to the "kiddie tax" rules. These tax implications need thorough evaluation to avoid unexpected liabilities and to optimize the tax strategy for the beneficiary's long-term benefit.

Selecting an appropriate custodian is another vital aspect that requires careful thought. The individual chosen to manage the custodianship account must be trustworthy, financially savvy, and willing to take on the responsibility. This decision should be approached with caution to prevent potential conflicts down the road. Naming a custodian involves considering their relationship with the child, their ability to manage finances prudently, and their willingness to follow the guidelines set forth by the original asset holder. Failure to choose the right custodian can lead to mismanagement of funds or disputes among family members, ultimately jeopardizing the minor's financial security.

Furthermore, it's important to acknowledge that custodianship arrangements might lack flexibility if circumstances change significantly over time. Life is unpredictable, and what seems like a fitting arrangement today may not hold up in the future. Changes in the financial market, shifts in the custodian's personal situation, or evolving needs of the minor can all necessitate adjustments that custodianship accounts may not easily accommodate. For example, if the selected custodian relocates to a different state with different laws regarding custodial accounts, this could complicate matters. Likewise, the minor's needs might change dramatically as they grow, requiring a more flexible approach to asset management than originally envisioned.

In addition to the above points, it's worth considering some practical guidelines when setting up custodianship accounts. Although guidelines will be covered in greater detail elsewhere, understanding the basics can help mitigate some of the discussed drawbacks. For instance, regularly reviewing and updating the custodial agreement ensures it remains relevant and aligned with the minor's best interests. Additionally, consulting with legal and financial advisors can offer insights into optimizing the structure and management of these accounts, addressing complex issues such as tax implications and asset suitability.

Choosing a Guardian

Selecting a guardian for minor children is a critical component of estate planning that ensures the continued welfare and financial security of the child in the event of untimely parental loss. The role of a guardian extends beyond merely providing shelter. A guardian becomes responsible for various aspects of the child's life, including education, healthcare, and overall well-being. This comprehensive responsibility necessitates careful consideration and diligent planning to select an appropriate individual who can step into this vital role.

When selecting a guardian, parents should prioritize individuals who align closely with their values and lifestyle choices. The guardian will be tasked with making significant decisions about the child's upbringing, such as educational paths, healthcare options, and moral guidance. Therefore, it is crucial to choose someone whose beliefs and daily habits reflect what the parents envision for their child's future. Additionally, the relationship between the prospective guardian and the child plays a pivotal role. A guardian who already has a strong, positive bond with the child may ease the emotional transition during a challenging time. This familiarity can provide a sense of continuity and stability, which is invaluable during periods of grief and adjustment.

Furthermore, the formalization of guardian selection is essential in legal documents such as wills or trusts. Including specific legal language detailing the chosen guardian's responsibilities can help prevent any ambiguities or disputes. Clear articulation of this designation not only underscores the parents' intentions but also provides the necessary legal backing to ensure these wishes are honored. Legal professionals often recommend consultations to craft precise language that adequately covers all anticipated scenarios and requirements.

Life is dynamic, and significant changes such as divorce, relocation, or other pivotal events may alter the suitability of the initially chosen guardian. Hence, it is advisable to periodically review and update guardian designations to reflect current circumstances. A periodic reassessment helps ensure that the selected guardian continues to be the best choice for the child's evolving needs and conditions. For example, a guardian who once lived nearby may have since moved to a different city or state, making it imperative to reconsider if they remain the optimal choice to provide daily support and care.

In many cases, families might initially overlook the importance of the guardian's financial acumen or ability to manage resources designated for the child's benefit. While love and relational proximity are paramount, overseeing financial matters – from managing inheritances to handling day-to-day expenses – requires a certain level of fiscal responsibility and knowledge. Parents need to feel confident that the chosen guardian can judiciously handle these responsibilities, ensuring the child's long-term financial well-being alongside their immediate physical and emotional needs.

Considerations about the guardian's age and health can also play a crucial role in the decision-making process. Older individuals, while dependable and affectionate, might face health challenges that could impede their ability to provide long-term care. Asking potential guardians about their willingness and capacity to take on such a substantial commitment is a conversation that parents cannot afford to bypass. Open dialogue about expectations and responsibilities ensures that everyone involved understands the gravity and longevity of the commitment being discussed.

Moreover, involving multiple family members in the discussion can foster a collective agreement and support network for the chosen guardian. In some instances, individuals may share guardianship duties, dividing responsibilities based on their strengths. For example, one might handle educational and health-related decisions, while another manages financial and extracurricular activities. Such an arrangement can ensure a more balanced and less burdensome guardianship, though it needs clear documentation to avoid misunderstandings and conflicts.

Delving further into legal considerations, crafting a will or trust with explicit instructions about the guardian's role mitigates the risk of legal challenges or familial disputes. Even in amicable families, lack of clarity can lead to disagreements, potentially prolonging court proceedings and causing unnecessary stress for the child. Including contingency plans within these documents can also be prudent. If the initially chosen guardian becomes unable or unwilling to serve, having secondary or alternate guardians predetermined ensures that there is no gap in the child's care.

Additionally, this legal framework should detail any specific directives regarding the child's upbringing. Clarifying preferences about education – whether prioritizing public schooling, private institutions, or home-schooling – healthcare choices, religious upbringing, and extra-curricular priorities can guide the guardian in aligning their care with the parents' original intentions. These provisions offer a roadmap that supports both the guardian and the child through the transition period and beyond.

Maintaining flexibility within the estate plan is also essential. As previously mentioned, life changes—whether personal circumstances like remarriage or broader issues such as changes in financial status—can influence the appropriateness of a chosen guardian. Regularly reviewing and updating the estate plan ensures it remains relevant and effective in safeguarding the child's interests. Scheduled reviews, perhaps every few years, can coincide with major life milestones to ensure timely updates.

In this chapter, we illuminated the critical role that custodianship accounts play in estate planning for families with minor children. These accounts provide a straightforward and effective means of managing assets until minors reach adulthood. By selecting responsible custodians and understanding the regulations surrounding these accounts, parents can ensure their children's financial needs are met for education, healthcare, and everyday living expenses. This approach helps avoid the cumbersome probate process, ensures funds are used appropriately, and offers peace of mind to both parents and guardians.

Additionally, the importance of choosing the right custodian cannot be overstated. The ideal custodian should be financially responsible, trustworthy, and capable of making sound decisions for the child's benefit. Establishing clear guidelines for managing the account and maintaining compliance with relevant laws adds another layer of security. By carefully considering all aspects of custodianship accounts and staying informed about potential limitations, families can create a robust plan that safeguards their children's financial future while simplifying the estate management process.

CHAPTER 8

Estate Planning for Special Needs Beneficiaries

Estate planning for special needs beneficiaries is a crucial aspect of securing the future for individuals with disabilities. This chapter focuses on various strategies to ensure that these beneficiaries receive the necessary financial support and quality of life enhancements without compromising their eligibility for essential government benefits. These strategies require careful considerations, both legal and personal, to address the unique needs of each individual while maintaining compliance with state and federal laws.

This chapter delves into specific tools, such as Special Needs Trusts (SNTs), which play a vital role in protecting the assets of disabled individuals without jeopardizing their access to Supplemental Security Income (SSI) and Medicaid. It covers the differences between self-settled and third-party trusts, guiding readers through the process of establishing these trusts, selecting suitable trustees, and managing them effectively. Additionally, the chapter addresses the intricacies of navigating government benefit regulations, ensuring accurate reporting, and staying informed about changes in legislation. Through detailed explanations and actionable advice, readers will gain invaluable insights into crafting comprehensive estate plans tailored to the needs of their loved ones with disabilities.

Special Needs Trusts

Special needs trusts (SNTs) play a crucial role in estate planning for individuals with disabilities. They are specialized tools designed to protect the assets of beneficiaries without jeopardizing their eligibility for government benefits such as Supplemental Security Income (SSI) and Medicaid. Understanding the purpose and functionality of these trusts is essential for families seeking to secure the financial future and enhance the quality of life for their loved ones with special needs.

A Special Needs Trust is a legal arrangement that allows individuals with disabilities to receive funds without compromising their eligibility for means-tested governmental aid. These trusts are established to manage resources for the benefit of the disabled individual, ensuring that they continue to qualify for government programs that provide vital support. The primary objective is to supplement the beneficiary's standard of living through personal care items, education, recreation, and other life-enhancing activities, without interfering with the public assistance they rely upon.

There are two main types of Special Needs Trusts: self-settled and third-party trusts. Self-settled trusts, also known as first-party trusts, are funded using the beneficiary's own assets. Often created from personal injury settlements or inheritances, these trusts must include a "payback" provision, stipulating that any remaining funds be used to reimburse the state for Medicaid benefits provided during the beneficiary's lifetime.

In contrast, third-party trusts are funded by assets belonging to someone other than the beneficiary, typically parents or grandparents. These trusts do not require a payback provision, allowing the remaining funds to be distributed to other family members or specified beneficiaries upon the death of the person with special needs. This flexibility makes third-party trusts a widely preferred option for many families planning long-term financial security for their loved ones with disabilities.

Establishing a Special Needs Trust involves several key steps and requires careful attention to legal requirements and documentation. The process begins by selecting the type of trust—either first-party or third-party—depending on the source of funding. Next, it is crucial to consult an attorney specializing in special needs estate planning to draft the trust document. This step ensures that the trust complies with federal and state laws, thereby protecting the beneficiary's eligibility for government benefits.

The trust document should clearly outline the purpose of the trust, name the trustee(s), and specify the terms under which the trust will operate. Funding the trust comes next, involving the transfer of assets into the trust. It is important to carefully consider which assets to include to maximize benefit and minimize tax implications. Following the initial setup, the trust must be administered according to its terms, adhering strictly to the guidelines set within.

Managing a Special Needs Trust successfully requires diligent oversight by the trustee. Trustees have a fiduciary duty to act in the best interest of the beneficiary, managing the trust's funds responsibly and ensuring compliance with all legal and reporting requirements. Best practices for trustees include maintaining clear and accurate records of all transactions, preparing annual accountings, and submitting necessary reports to the appropriate state agencies.

Trustees should also be well-versed in the specific needs and preferences of the beneficiary, making disbursements that improve their quality of life while preserving eligibility for essential government benefits. Communication with the beneficiary and their caregivers is paramount to ensure that the trust's resources are utilized effectively and responsibly.

Ongoing education and training for trustees can further enhance their ability to manage the SNT effectively. Numerous resources, including workshops, online courses, and consultation with legal and financial advisors, are available to help trustees fulfill their responsibilities. Regular review and adjustment of the trust's strategy may be necessary to respond to changes in the beneficiary's circumstances or alterations in relevant laws and regulations.

Government Benefit Considerations

Understanding how estate planning impacts eligibility for government benefits is crucial when planning for special needs beneficiaries. This discussion begins with a focus on means-tested benefits, which are pivotal to the financial security and well-being of individuals with disabilities.

Means-tested benefits, such as Supplemental Security Income (SSI) and Medicaid, provide essential support to individuals with special needs. SSI offers monthly payments to disabled individuals who have limited income and resources, helping cover daily living expenses. Medicaid provides health coverage for low-income individuals, ensuring access to necessary medical care and long-term services. The primary eligibility criteria for both programs hinge on income and asset limits. For instance, an individual must typically have less than $2,000 in countable assets to qualify for SSI. Understanding these thresholds is vital because exceeding the limits can lead to disqualification from benefits, causing significant financial jeopardy.

Navigating the interaction between trusts and government benefits is another critical aspect of estate planning for special needs beneficiaries. A Special Needs Trust (SNT) can be structured to hold assets for a beneficiary without impacting their eligibility for means-tested benefits. This type of trust allows parents or guardians to set aside funds for the benefit of their loved one while ensuring the funds do not count as available resources under SSI and Medicaid rules. Properly drafted SNTs can pay for goods and services not covered by government programs, such as education, therapy, transportation, and recreational activities.

However, it's essential to structure these trusts correctly to avoid disqualification from benefits. For example, trusts should be irrevocable and managed by a trustee other than the beneficiary to ensure compliance with regulations. Legal professionals specializing in special needs planning can provide guidance on setting up these trusts, taking into account the specifics of state and federal laws. Consistent review and adjustment of the trust are also necessary to accommodate changing laws and regulations that may affect the trust's operation and the beneficiary's eligibility for government assistance.

Accurate reporting is another cornerstone of maintaining eligibility for benefits. Program administrators require regular updates on the beneficiary's financial status and any changes in income or assets. Failure to report changes accurately and timely can result in penalties, including the suspension or termination of benefits. Beneficiaries and their families need to maintain meticulous records and documentation to ensure they comply with reporting obligations. This includes keeping receipts for expenditures paid from the trust and documenting all income sources.

Examples of common reporting requirements include annual recertification for SSI recipients, where beneficiaries must report any change in living arrangements, income, and resources. Medicaid may require periodic reviews to verify continued eligibility based on income and resource levels. Families should work closely with caregivers, financial advisors, and attorneys to ensure that they understand and meet these reporting requirements consistently.

Changes in legislation also play a significant role in estate planning for special needs beneficiaries. Laws governing means-tested benefits and special needs trusts are subject to change, and staying informed about these changes is imperative. For example, changes to Social Security regulations or state Medicaid rules can impact the funding and distribution of trusts, necessitating adjustments to estate planning strategies.

Keeping abreast of legislative updates involves monitoring relevant government and legal resources. Families can subscribe to newsletters from disability advocacy organizations, join support groups, and consult with legal experts specializing in special needs planning. Regular consultations with professionals can help anticipate and respond to changes in the legal landscape, ensuring that estate plans remain effective and compliant with current laws.

Trustee Selection

Choosing the right trustee for a special needs trust is one of the most critical decisions in estate planning for individuals with disabilities. This role requires not only financial acumen but also a deep understanding of the unique challenges faced by those with special needs. Selecting someone who possesses these qualities will help ensure that the beneficiary's financial security and quality of life are maintained.

The first step in selecting a trustee is to evaluate key characteristics that make someone suitable for this important role. Financial acumen is paramount since managing a trust involves handling investments, budgeting, and making financial decisions. A trustee must have a solid grasp of financial principles and be able to seek and interpret professional advice when necessary. Additionally, interpersonal skills are crucial as trustees often need to interact with beneficiaries, their families, and various professionals. They should be empathetic, patient, and effective communicators.

Another essential characteristic is an understanding of special needs challenges. Trustees need to be familiar with the specific needs of the beneficiary, including medical, educational, and social requirements. This awareness helps ensure that the trust funds are used appropriately and beneficially. Without this understanding, even a financially savvy trustee may struggle to prioritize expenses that significantly impact the beneficiary's well-being.

When considering who to appoint as a trustee, several options can be evaluated: family members, professionals, and corporate trustees. Each has its own benefits and drawbacks. Family members often have intimate knowledge of the beneficiary's needs and preferences, making them emotionally invested and more likely to act in the individual's best interest. However, they may lack the necessary financial expertise or could become overwhelmed by the responsibilities involved, which might lead to potential conflicts within the family.

Professionals, such as lawyers or accountants, bring a high level of financial competence and experience in managing trusts. They can provide objective and knowledgeable oversight, ensuring compliance with legal and financial requirements. Yet, their services come at a cost, and they may not have an in-depth understanding of the beneficiary's personal circumstances unless they take extra steps to become informed.

Corporate trustees, typically financial institutions, combine professional management with robust systems for handling large sums of money. They offer reliability, continuity, and extensive resources. The downside is that corporate trustees may lack the personal touch and flexibility that families sometimes need, and they might be more expensive than individual trustees.

Training and support are vital components in ensuring that trustees perform their duties effectively. Resources such as legal advisors, workshops, and online courses can provide invaluable guidance. Legal advisors can help trustees navigate the complex regulatory landscape and ensure compliance with relevant laws. Workshops may offer practical, hands-on training and opportunities to learn from real-life scenarios. Online courses offer a convenient way to stay updated on best practices and emerging trends in trust management. Utilizing these resources can significantly enhance a trustee's ability to manage special needs trusts competently.

Moreover, it is crucial to prepare for unexpected circumstances by having contingency plans for trustee changes. Life is unpredictable, and situations may arise where a trustee can no longer fulfill their duties due to illness, relocation, or other personal reasons. Establishing clear mechanisms for replacing trustees ensures that the trust continues to operate smoothly without interruption. This might involve naming successor trustees within the trust document, thereby providing a seamless transition of responsibilities. Contingency planning also includes periodic reviews of the trustee's performance and the overall administration of the trust, allowing adjustments to be made before issues escalate.

Letter of Intent

A letter of intent is a cornerstone in estate planning for special needs beneficiaries. It's not a legally binding document but holds immense value in providing detailed guidance about the care and preferences of a special needs individual. Essentially, it serves as a roadmap for future caregivers and trustees, helping to ensure continuity and consistency in the beneficiary's care.

One crucial aspect of a letter of intent is its purpose. This document communicates essential information that might not be reflected in legal estate planning documents. It covers personal details on the day-to-day care, routines, preferences, and needs of the special needs individual, ensuring they receive consistent and tailored care even if their primary caregiver is no longer able to provide it. For instance, a letter of intent might outline the individual's daily schedule, preferred activities, dietary restrictions, and specific medical treatments, which can significantly aid those who will take over the caregiving role.

Moving on to the elements of a comprehensive letter of intent, it should encapsulate several critical areas. First, medical needs must be clearly documented. This includes any diagnoses, medications, therapies, and the names and contact information of healthcare providers. Having this information readily available ensures that medical care remains uninterrupted and accurately administered according to the established treatment plans.

Routine and lifestyle information is equally vital. Detailing daily and weekly routines helps caregivers maintain a sense of normalcy and stability for the beneficiary. For example, noting the best times for certain activities, like morning routines or bedtime rituals, can make transitions smoother for both the caregivers and the individual with special needs.

Emotional support strategies are another key component. Special needs individuals often benefit from specific emotional and behavioral interventions. Capturing these in a letter of intent helps new caregivers understand how to effectively communicate and interact with the beneficiary. This might include preferred methods of calming the individual, rewarding positive behavior, or managing anxiety and stress.

Additionally, the letter should list important contacts, such as family members, friends, therapists, and educators, along with their roles in the individual's life. This network of relationships is integral to the beneficiary's well-being and can offer support and familiarity during periods of change.

Updating the letter of intent regularly cannot be overstated. Estate planners should review and update the letter after significant life changes, such as shifts in medical needs, changes in caregivers, or adjustments in living arrangements. These updates ensure that the document remains relevant and continues to serve its purpose effectively. For instance, if the beneficiary begins a new therapeutic regimen or moves to a different residential setting, these changes need timely documentation.

Finally, sharing the letter of intent is an important step. While maintaining confidentiality is essential, appropriate parties, including family members, trustees, and close friends, should have access to the letter to ensure they can fulfill their respective roles effectively. It's also beneficial to discuss the contents of the letter with those involved so they fully understand the nuances of the care plan and can ask any clarifying questions.

Ensuring Financial Security and Quality of Life

Ensuring financial security and enhancing the quality of life for special needs beneficiaries are key goals when planning an estate. This requires thoughtful consideration of various funding sources, structuring trust distributions wisely, aligning activities with the beneficiary's interests, and adhering to legal requirements.

Funding Sources for Special Needs Trusts

A critical component in establishing a special needs trust is identifying appropriate funding sources. Common methods include personal assets, which might consist of savings, investments, or real estate. These assets can provide immediate and long-term support for the beneficiary. Additionally, parents and guardians often consider life insurance policies as a reliable funding source. By designating the trust as the beneficiary of their life insurance policy, they can ensure that funds will be available to support their child's needs after their passing. Moreover, some families leverage retirement accounts and pensions by allocating portions of these funds to the trust. Each of these funding options provides unique benefits and can be tailored to meet the specific needs of the beneficiary.

Structuring Trust Distributions

Properly structuring trust distributions is vital to maintain eligibility for government benefits such as Supplemental Security Income (SSI) and Medicaid. Distributions should be planned strategically to ensure that they do not exceed resource limits set by these programs. For example, paying directly for goods and services such as medical equipment, therapy, or educational expenses can benefit the individual without affecting benefit eligibility. Trustees must understand the types of distributions that are considered "in-kind support" and are countable under SSI rules. Therefore, it's important to strike a balance between meeting the beneficiary's needs and preserving their access to essential government assistance.

One strategy to maximize the effectiveness of trust distributions while maintaining benefits is to utilize third-party payments for items beneficial to the beneficiary but not disqualifying them from benefits. Examples include direct payments for medical bills, education, and home improvements that specifically cater to the special needs individual. The trustee should regularly review the beneficiary's government benefits and adapt the distribution strategy to avoid accidental disqualification.

Aligning With Beneficiary's Interests

A successful special needs trust doesn't just focus on financial security; it also considers the beneficiary's quality of life and personal preferences. The trustee must have a deep understanding of the beneficiary's interests, hobbies, and long-term goals. This alignment ensures that the trust funds are used in ways that genuinely enhance the beneficiary's daily life. For instance, if the beneficiary enjoys art, the trust could fund art classes or purchase supplies. If they benefit from particular therapies or recreational activities, the trust can prioritize these expenditures. Regular communication with the beneficiary and their close family members is essential to stay informed about their evolving needs and interests.

Tailoring the trust's activities to the beneficiary's preferences not only improves their quality of life but also fosters a sense of independence and fulfillment. A person-centered approach encourages the trustee to invest in experiences and services that foster growth, happiness, and well-being. Moreover, incorporating the beneficiary's voice in decision-making processes whenever possible adds to their sense of autonomy and respect.

Legal Compliance

Adhering to relevant laws and regulations is imperative in order to maintain the trust's validity and the beneficiary's eligibility for government support. Trusts must comply with federal and state laws governing special needs trusts, including correct drafting, proper administration, and periodic reporting. Ensuring the trust remains compliant with these legal standards prevents costly legal disputes and potential loss of benefits.

Trustees need to be well-versed in both the requirements for special needs trusts and any changes in legislation that may affect the trust. Staying updated on new laws and regulations helps trustees adjust their strategies accordingly. For example, the Social Security Administration (SSA) occasionally updates its guidelines regarding resources and income for SSI recipients. The trustee must promptly respond to such changes to avoid jeopardizing the beneficiary's benefits.

Understanding and fulfilling reporting obligations is another critical aspect. Trusts are often required to provide annual accountings to courts or other oversight bodies. Accurate records of all transactions, including receipts and expenditures, must be maintained meticulously. Furthermore, trustees must ensure that tax filings for the trust are accurate and submitted on time, avoiding unnecessary penalties or complications.

Lastly, it is advisable for trustees to work closely with legal professionals specializing in special needs trust law. Legal counsel can provide guidance on complex issues and assist in navigating the myriad requirements associated with managing a special needs trust. Engaging with knowledgeable attorneys ensures that all aspects of the trust are handled correctly, safeguarding both the trust and the beneficiary's interests.

This chapter underscored the importance of tailoring estate planning strategies to address the unique needs of individuals with disabilities. By establishing Special Needs Trusts and understanding government benefit considerations, families can ensure that their loved ones with special needs receive the necessary financial support without compromising their eligibility for crucial programs like SSI and Medicaid. Additionally, selecting an appropriate trustee and crafting a detailed letter of intent are vital steps in safeguarding the beneficiary's quality of life and ensuring continuity in their care.

Incorporating these specialized tools and approaches into estate planning helps secure the financial future of individuals with disabilities while promoting their overall well-being. Families must stay informed about legal requirements and remain diligent in managing trust resources effectively. With careful planning and ongoing education, estate planners can create robust frameworks that provide both financial security and an enhanced quality of life for their special needs beneficiaries, thus fulfilling their long-term goals and aspirations.

CHAPTER 9

Business Succession Planning

Determining the value of a business is a critical component in the realm of business succession planning. Understanding the accurate worth of a business lays the foundation for smooth transitions and ensures that financial outcomes are beneficial for successors. It aids in maintaining the legacy built by the original owner and ensures continuity of operations, paving the way for the future leadership of the enterprise.

In this chapter, various methods of business valuation will be explored, including income-based, market-based, and asset-based approaches. The role of professional appraisers in achieving accurate valuations will also be highlighted. Additionally, the importance of proper documentation for legal and tax purposes will be discussed, ensuring compliance and preventing potential disputes. By delving into these strategies, readers will gain actionable insights to secure the longevity and success of their businesses through well-informed succession planning.

Valuing Your Business

A fundamental aspect of business succession planning is accurately determining the value of a business. This process is crucial as it informs decisions related to the transition, ensuring that financial outcomes are optimized for successors. Proper valuation of a business secures its future by providing a clear understanding of its worth, facilitating smoother ownership transitions, and safeguarding the legacy built by the original owner.

To begin with, there are several methods for assessing business value, which can vary significantly depending on market performance and industry standards. One common approach is the income-based method, which calculates the present value of expected future earnings. This method relies heavily on financial projections and discount rates and may be most appropriate for businesses with stable and predictable cash flows. Another widely used technique is the market-based method, which compares the business to similar companies that have been recently sold in the same industry. This comparative analysis provides a benchmark based on actual market data, reflecting what buyers are willing to pay under current economic conditions. Lastly, the asset-based method focuses on the business's tangible and intangible assets and liabilities, essentially determining the net value of the company if everything were liquidated. Each of these methods has distinct advantages and limitations, and choosing the right one depends on the specific characteristics of the business being valued.

Engaging the services of professional business appraisers or valuation experts is another critical step in obtaining an accurate assessment. These professionals possess the necessary expertise and experience to conduct thorough valuations, utilizing advanced techniques and industry knowledge. They can provide a comprehensive analysis that includes reviewing financial statements, conducting market research, and applying appropriate valuation methods. By leveraging their expertise, business owners can ensure a precise and credible valuation, which is essential for making informed succession planning decisions. Furthermore, these experts can identify any potential issues or considerations that might affect the final valuation, such as economic conditions, industry trends, or regulatory changes.

The valuation of a business significantly impacts the buy-in and motivation of potential successors. A well-determined value ensures that successors understand the true worth of the business, fostering transparency and trust. Potential successors are more likely to commit to the transition if they perceive the valuation process as fair and objective. Additionally, knowing the accurate value of the business can help successors plan their finances and secure necessary funding if they need to purchase ownership stakes. This clarity can also prevent conflicts among family members or partners by providing an objective basis for negotiations and agreements. In some cases, successors might be motivated to take on leadership roles within the company, seeing the potential for growth and profitability based on the valuation.

Documenting valuation methods and results is paramount for legal and tax purposes. Proper documentation ensures compliance with relevant laws and regulations, reducing the risk of disputes or legal challenges. When the valuation process is meticulously recorded, it provides a transparent trail that can be referenced during audits, legal proceedings, or ownership transitions. For tax purposes, the documented valuation serves as a basis for calculating taxes owed on the transfer of ownership. This is especially important in estate planning, where inaccuracies in valuation could lead to significant tax liabilities for heirs or successors. Adequate documentation also enhances the credibility of the valuation, ensuring that all stakeholders recognize its legitimacy.

Succession Options

When planning for business succession, one crucial aspect to consider is the potential benefits and challenges of passing the business to family members. This approach is often emotionally appealing as it allows the business owner to keep the enterprise within the family, potentially preserving its legacy for generations. There are several clear benefits to this option. It may offer financial security for family members who depend on the business for their livelihood. Additionally, family members might be more dedicated to maintaining the success and values of the business since they have a personal stake in its continuity.

However, this approach also comes with significant challenges. For one, not all family members may be equally interested or capable of running the business effectively. There could be disparities in skills, experience, or even enthusiasm, which can lead to internal conflicts. Moreover, handing over the reins to family members without proper preparation can result in poor business decisions and management issues. It's essential to ensure that family members who are taking over possess the necessary capability and are adequately trained. Establishing clear roles and responsibilities can help mitigate some of these challenges, ensuring a smoother transition.

Another viable option for succession is selling the business to current employees or partners. This strategy can be beneficial because existing employees and partners already understand the operational intricacies of the business. Their familiarity with the company's culture, customers, and processes means they can often maintain continuity with minimal disruption. Selling the business to an internal party can also boost employee morale, as they may feel more invested in the company's success when they have an ownership stake.

However, this method has its own set of obstacles. Financing the purchase can be a significant hurdle. Employees or partners may lack sufficient funds to buy the business outright, necessitating creative financing solutions such as installment payments, profit-sharing arrangements, or external loans. Furthermore, transitioning from colleagues to owners can create new dynamics and potentially lead to conflicts if not managed correctly. Clear agreements and open communication are vital to overcoming these challenges, ensuring a smooth and equitable transfer.

Evaluating the prospect of selling the business to an outsider is another succession route worth considering. This approach can often provide the highest financial return, as it opens up the market to potential buyers who may place a higher value on the business. Selling to an outsider can be particularly advantageous if the goal is to maximize the financial outcome rather than ensuring continuity within the family or among current employees.

Nonetheless, selling to an outsider also presents unique challenges. Finding the right buyer who aligns with the business's values and objectives can be time-consuming. There's also the risk that the new owner may make significant changes that could disrupt existing operations or alter the company culture. To mitigate these risks, it's essential to engage in thorough vetting processes and possibly negotiate terms that protect certain aspects of the business during the transition period.

Working with experienced brokers or advisors can help navigate these complexities and secure a favorable deal.

An overarching element crucial to all succession options is the importance of creating detailed business continuity plans. Such plans act as roadmaps to ensure a smooth transition regardless of the chosen succession strategy. They typically include comprehensive details about operational procedures, key contacts, financial information, and contingency plans for various scenarios. These plans help maintain stability and ensure that the business can continue to operate seamlessly during and after the transition.

A well-crafted business continuity plan should outline the steps needed to prepare successors for their new roles. This might involve training programs, mentorship opportunities, and gradual handovers of responsibility. Additionally, the plan should detail how to communicate the transition to employees, customers, and other stakeholders. Clear communication helps manage expectations and minimizes uncertainty, which can be critical in maintaining trust and loyalty during the transition period.

Moreover, regular reviews and updates to the business continuity plan are essential. As the business environment and market conditions evolve, so too should the strategies for ensuring a smooth transition. Periodic evaluations allow adjustments to be made, keeping the plan relevant and effective in addressing current realities. This ongoing process helps safeguard the business against unforeseen challenges and ensures that it remains resilient through leadership changes.

Ultimately, selecting the best succession approach depends on the unique circumstances of each business owner. Whether passing the business to family members, selling to employees or partners, or opting for an external sale, each path offers distinct advantages and hurdles. Thoroughly evaluating these options, along with crafting and updating a robust business continuity plan, will aid business owners in making informed decisions that protect their legacy and secure the future of their enterprises.

Buy-Sell Agreements

In the realm of business succession planning, buy-sell agreements play a pivotal role. They establish a clear and reliable framework for the transfer of business ownership upon the occurrence of specific triggering events, such as retirement, death, or disability of an owner. Understanding their necessity can help ensure a smooth transition and maintain the stability and continuity of the business.

To begin with, buy-sell agreements are legal contracts that outline the terms and conditions under which business interests may be transferred. These agreements serve not only to protect the interests of current owners but also to provide a structured path for future ownership changes. By having a buy-sell agreement in place, businesses can avoid potential conflicts and disruptions that could arise from unforeseen circumstances.

Buy-sell agreements come in various forms, each suited to different needs and situations. Two primary types are cross-purchase agreements and entity-purchase agreements.

In a cross-purchase agreement, individual owners agree to purchase the shares of a departing owner. This type is typically used in small businesses where there are few owners. Each owner purchases life insurance policies on the other owners, ensuring that funds are available to buy out the shares if one owner passes away. This arrangement helps maintain balance and control within the remaining ownership structure and avoids involving external parties.

Entity-purchase agreements, on the other hand, involve the business entity itself buying back the shares of a departing owner. Also known as redemption agreements, these are more common in larger businesses with multiple owners. The business typically takes out life insurance policies on the owners, and the proceeds are used to redeem the shares of a deceased or disabled owner. This method simplifies the process for the remaining owners as it consolidates the buyout within the business rather than among individual owners.

Funding buy-sell agreements is a crucial aspect that requires careful consideration. Among the most popular funding options is life insurance. Life insurance provides a reliable source of funds to meet the financial obligations of a buy-sell agreement upon the death of an owner. Term life insurance is often used for its lower premiums, while permanent life insurance might be preferred for its cash value component, which can be accessed during the owner's lifetime if necessary.

Savings or sinking funds present another option. Businesses can set aside money gradually over time to cover future buyouts. This approach offers flexibility, as the saved funds can be used for various purposes if the triggering event does not occur. However, it requires disciplined saving and may not provide the immediate liquidity that life insurance offers.

While less common, borrowing is also an option. In this scenario, the business or remaining owners take out a loan to fund the buyout. Though this can provide the needed capital, it introduces debt into the equation and might burden the business with repayment obligations.

Drafting an effective buy-sell agreement necessitates professional legal advice. Given the complex nature of these contracts and the significant impact they have on the future of the business, consulting with legal experts ensures that all relevant factors and potential scenarios are thoroughly considered. Legal professionals can tailor the agreement to fit the unique needs of the business, covering essential details such as valuation methods, terms of payment, and dispute resolution mechanisms.

Moreover, legal advice is invaluable in navigating the nuances of state laws and tax implications associated with buy-sell agreements. Different jurisdictions may have varying regulations, and thorough legal guidance helps ensure compliance and optimized tax outcomes. For instance, structuring the agreement in a tax-efficient manner can minimize tax liabilities for both the departing owner and the remaining owners, preserving the business's financial health.

Leadership Continuity Plans

Ensuring leadership continuity is crucial for the longevity and success of a business. A well-thought-out leadership continuity plan helps guarantee that capable leadership is in place during and after the transition period, safeguarding the business's legacy and future growth.

The first step in establishing a leadership continuity plan is identifying potential successors within the organization. Begin by evaluating employees who demonstrate strong leadership qualities, technical competence, and a deep understanding of the company's vision and values. This involves conducting regular performance reviews, seeking feedback from peers and subordinates, and assessing individual capabilities through various scenarios. It's important to consider both current contributions and future potential when selecting candidates for leadership roles.

Once potential successors have been identified, the next step is to develop a structured training program tailored to their needs. This program should encompass both formal and informal methods of learning. Formal training can include external courses, workshops, and certifications relevant to the business and industry. Informal training might involve mentoring and coaching sessions with current leaders, on-the-job training, and rotating assignments to expose candidates to different aspects of the business. The goal is to equip successors with the necessary skills and knowledge to handle leadership responsibilities effectively.

A phased transition of leadership responsibilities ensures a smooth operation during the succession process. This approach allows successors to gradually acclimate to their new roles while gaining valuable experience under the guidance of existing leaders. Start by delegating minor tasks and decision-making authority, then progressively increase their responsibilities over time. This phased approach not only eases the transition for the successors but also minimizes disruptions to the business operations. Regularly scheduled meetings between outgoing and incoming leaders can facilitate knowledge transfer and provide opportunities to address any challenges that may arise.

Ongoing monitoring and adjustment of leadership continuity plans are essential to their effectiveness. The business environment is dynamic, and unexpected changes can occur. Therefore, it is critical to periodically review and update the continuity plan based on current circumstances and long-term goals. Establishing key performance indicators (KPIs) to measure the progress and readiness of potential successors is one way to ensure continuous improvement. Additionally, gathering feedback from various stakeholders, including employees, customers, and board members, can offer valuable insights into how well the leadership transition is being managed.

Key Legal and Financial Considerations

Ensuring a smooth transition of business ownership and management requires careful consideration of both legal and financial implications. One of the primary aspects involves addressing key legal considerations such as wills, trusts, and overall estate planning. To protect the legacy of your business, it is essential to have a well-drafted will outlining how the business assets should be distributed upon the owner's death. A will serves as the cornerstone of an estate plan, ensuring that the business is transferred according to the owner's wishes and avoiding potential disputes among heirs.

Trusts offer another layer of security and flexibility in succession planning. By placing business assets into a trust, owners can stipulate specific terms for the management and distribution of these assets, providing for a smoother and more controlled transition. Trusts can help avoid probate, reduce estate taxes, and ensure continued operation without interruption. For example, a revocable living trust allows the business owner to maintain control over the business during their lifetime while designating successor trustees who will take over management seamlessly in event of incapacity or death.

Estate planning also encompasses other important documents like power of attorney and healthcare directives. These documents ensure that trusted individuals are authorized to make critical decisions on behalf of the business owner in case of incapacitation, thus maintaining continuity in operations during unforeseen circumstances.

Another significant factor in business succession planning is understanding the impact of tax regulations. Transitioning a business involves various tax implications, including estate taxes, capital gains taxes, and gift taxes. Business owners need to be aware of these potential liabilities and plan accordingly to mitigate their effects. For instance, federal estate taxes can take a substantial portion of the business's value if not planned for properly, potentially forcing heirs to sell parts of the business to cover the tax burden.

Strategies for minimizing tax burdens during ownership transfers include leveraging gifting strategies, valuation discounts, and utilising family limited partnerships. Gifting shares of the business incrementally can help reduce the taxable estate, taking advantage of annual gift tax exclusions. Additionally, valuation discounts for minority interests or lack of marketability can lower the overall value subjected to estate taxes, making the transition more tax-efficient.

Family Limited Partnerships (FLPs) are another effective tool in minimizing tax burdens. By transferring business assets into an FLP, owners can retain control while gradually transferring ownership to their heirs. The value of partnership interests can often be discounted for gift and estate tax purposes, leading to significant tax savings. However, it's essential to consult with a knowledgeable tax advisor or estate planner to navigate these complex strategies successfully.

The role of financial planning in securing a stable future for the business and its successors cannot be overstated. Financial planning ensures that the business remains viable and prosperous throughout the transition period and beyond. A comprehensive financial plan includes liquidity analysis, assessing the business's cash flow needs, and ensuring there are sufficient funds available to cover operational costs, taxes, and other expenses during the transition.

One practical approach is setting up a buy-sell agreement funded by life insurance. This arrangement ensures that funds are readily available to purchase the deceased owner's interest in the business, providing financial stability for both the business and the owner's family. Life insurance proceeds can provide the necessary liquidity, preventing the need to sell business assets at a potentially undervalued rate.

Moreover, diversifying investment portfolios and creating reserve funds can buffer against economic downturns or unexpected expenses during the transition. Succession planning should also include a thorough review of the business's financial health and performance metrics. Regular financial audits and evaluations help identify potential areas of improvement, ensuring that the business remains attractive and profitable for future generations.

In addition to internal financial planning, seeking external advice from financial advisors, accountants, and attorneys specializing in succession planning can provide valuable insights and strategies tailored to the unique needs of the business. Professional advisors can help navigate complex legal and financial landscapes, ensuring compliance with all regulations and optimizing the transition process.

This chapter provided essential strategies for ensuring a smooth transition of business ownership and management. By accurately determining the value of a business, owners can secure their legacy and ensure continuity. Various valuation methods such as income-based, market-based, and asset-based offer tailored approaches depending on the business's characteristics. Engaging professional appraisers aids in obtaining precise valuations, fostering trust and transparency among potential successors. Proper documentation of valuation methods also addresses legal and tax requirements, safeguarding against disputes.

Succession planning options were explored, highlighting the benefits and challenges of passing the business to family members, current employees, or outsiders. Each option requires detailed consideration to align with the owner's goals and business needs. Creating a robust business continuity plan ensures seamless operations during transitions. Regular reviews and updates are crucial to maintain relevance amidst changing market conditions. Ultimately, informed decisions bolstered by strategic planning protect the business's legacy and support its future growth.

CHAPTER 10

Digital Asset Management

Digital Asset Management plays a vital role in modern estate planning, focusing on the secure inclusion and management of digital assets. As technology continues to evolve at a rapid pace, understanding the scope and significance of digital assets becomes essential for anyone looking to safeguard their legacy. This chapter addresses the concept of digital assets and underscores the importance of integrating these intangible yet valuable elements into an overall estate plan. By appreciating the breadth of digital assets—which range from social media accounts to cryptocurrencies—individuals can better prepare to manage and protect them effectively.

In this chapter, readers will explore various categories of digital assets, such as personal, financial, and professional, to gain clarity on what needs attention within their estate plans. The chapter also delves into the methods for assessing the value of digital assets and emphasizes the importance of proper documentation to prevent disputes and facilitate access for heirs. Additionally, actionable steps are provided to help individuals identify their digital assets, categorize them for easier management, and conduct regular updates to keep the inventory current. By the end of this chapter, readers will be equipped with comprehensive strategies to ensure that their online presence is seamlessly integrated into their legacy management strategy.

Identifying Digital Assets

Digital Asset Management is a crucial aspect of modern estate planning, ensuring that digital assets are securely included and properly managed. As technology continues to evolve, understanding what constitutes a digital asset becomes essential for individuals seeking to protect their legacy. This subpoint aims to help readers recognize various digital assets and understand why including them in an estate plan is vital.

Digital assets encompass a broad array of items, ranging from social media accounts, emails, and online banking credentials to cryptocurrencies and digital music libraries. These assets can hold significant sentimental or financial value. For instance, a popular social media account might contain years of cherished memories and interactions, while a cryptocurrency wallet could represent a substantial portion of one's net worth. Identifying these assets early in the estate planning process helps ensure they are properly managed and protected.

Understanding different types of digital assets reveals numerous opportunities for legacy planning. By categorizing assets into personal, financial, and professional, one can better identify what needs attention. Personal digital assets include email accounts, social media profiles, and photos stored online. Financial digital assets consist of online banking accounts, investment portfolios, and cryptocurrencies like Bitcoin or Ethereum. Professional digital assets encompass business-related data, domain names, and work-related digital files. Recognizing these categories can clarify what requires management and protection, making the estate planning process more comprehensive.

Valuing digital assets is another critical aspect of proper estate planning. The valuation influences how assets are distributed to heirs and contributes to an accurate calculation of net worth. Cryptocurrencies, for example, have become increasingly valuable, with some individuals possessing portfolios worth thousands or even millions of dollars. Accurately assessing the value of cryptocurrencies ensures equitable distribution among beneficiaries. Additionally, understanding the worth of other digital assets, such as domain names or online businesses, ensures that these assets contribute appropriately to the overall estate valuation.

Proper documentation of digital assets is paramount to prevent disputes among beneficiaries and facilitate easier access for heirs. Creating a comprehensive inventory of digital assets, complete with usernames, passwords, and security questions, ensures that appointed individuals can manage these assets effectively. Including instructions on how assets should be handled after one's passing, such as whether a social media account should be memorialized or deleted, can prevent confusion and potential conflicts among heirs. Documentation should also include stipulations for accessing online banking accounts and investment portfolios, ensuring a smooth transition of financial responsibilities.

To assist readers in identifying their digital assets, begin by listing all online services and accounts you use frequently. This includes social media profiles, email accounts, subscriptions, and cloud storage services. Next, compile information about any digital currencies or online bank accounts you possess. Don't forget to consider less obvious assets, such as digital music or book libraries and any intellectual property stored online. Once this initial list is created, categorize each item into personal, financial, or professional assets for easier management.

Assessing the value of your digital assets may seem daunting, but it's a necessary step in estate planning. For tangible digital assets like cryptocurrencies, track their market value regularly since values can fluctuate widely. For less tangible items, such as social media accounts, consider their sentimental value and any potential revenue they generate. Consulting with financial advisors who specialize in digital assets can provide clarity on the monetary worth of online businesses or investments, ensuring an accurate assessment.

Documentation is more than just recording usernames and passwords; it involves creating a structured plan for managing digital assets. Start by using secure password managers to store login details safely. Document any two-factor authentication methods used for additional security. Explicitly state your wishes for each asset, whether it should be preserved, transferred, or deleted. Ensure that trusted individuals, such as executors or family members, know where and how to access this information. Regularly update this documentation to reflect any changes in your digital footprint.

Updating your list of digital assets periodically is vital due to the dynamic nature of the digital landscape. Schedule annual reviews to add new accounts or remove obsolete ones. This proactive approach ensures no assets are overlooked and maintains an up-to-date inventory. During these reviews, verify that accessible information remains current, and adjust valuations as needed to reflect market changes or personal circumstances.

Access and Control Issues

Digital assets, from social media accounts to online banking and cryptocurrencies, have become an integral part of our lives. However, the complexities involved in managing these assets after someone passes away or becomes incapacitated are often underestimated. This subpoint delves into the intricate challenges faced when trying to access and control digital assets under such circumstances.

One of the primary hurdles is the varying policies of different platforms for accessing the accounts of deceased users. Each platform, be it Facebook, Google, or online banking services, has its own set of rules that must be followed. Some may require legal documentation such as a death certificate or proof of authority, while others might provide options for memorializing accounts instead of full access. It's crucial to be familiar with these common practices to streamline the recovery process and avoid unnecessary delays.

For instance, Facebook allows profiles to be memorialized, which freezes the account but keeps it accessible to friends and family. On the other hand, Google offers an Inactive Account Manager tool, where users can specify who should gain access to their accounts if they remain inactive for a certain period. Understanding and utilizing these tools can significantly ease the stress of dealing with digital assets during an already challenging emotional time.

Privacy concerns present another significant obstacle. Digital privacy laws can vary greatly depending on the jurisdiction, adding layers of complexity. Legal restrictions often govern who can access an individual's digital records and under what conditions. Matters become even more complicated when considering international platforms and data stored across borders. It's pivotal to navigate these issues carefully to ensure compliance and avoid unintentional breaches of privacy.

Addressing privacy concerns also means understanding the limitations imposed by terms of service agreements. Many online platforms outline specific conditions under which user information can be shared posthumously. Navigating these terms requires a thorough understanding to ensure that loved ones aren't left in the dark about essential digital assets.

To mitigate the risk of these complications, a proactive approach involves implementing a system where trusted individuals are designated to access one's digital assets. Including clear directives within estate planning documents such as wills and trusts can prevent potential legal disputes and ensure smooth transitions. This strategy not only provides clarity to executors and beneficiaries but also protects against unauthorized access.

Appointing a digital executor – someone explicitly charged with managing digital assets – can be particularly effective. This person would handle everything from closing email accounts to distributing any monetary value tied to digital properties. By specifying roles and responsibilities beforehand, you reduce ambiguity and the chances of conflict among heirs.

Emphasizing preparedness further, leveraging technology can greatly enhance the management and security of digital assets. Digital vaults, for example, offer a secure way to store crucial account details, passwords, and sensitive information. These vaults serve as repositories where all essential digital data can be kept together, providing easy access to authorized individuals when necessary.

Digital vaults come equipped with robust encryption and stringent security protocols, ensuring that sensitive information remains protected from unauthorized access. They can include features like automatic data backups and multi-factor authentication, enhancing overall reliability. Knowing that valuable digital assets are protected in this way can offer peace of mind and substantially simplify the estate planning process.

Beyond just storage, technology can assist in automating aspects of digital asset management. Tools that track digital footprints and monitor activity can alert appointed persons about any required actions, helping maintain organized oversight. For instance, smartphone applications can remind users to update their digital inventory regularly, ensuring that vital information remains current and comprehensive.

The importance of educating oneself and staying informed cannot be overstated. As technologies evolve, so do the measures required to manage them effectively. Continuous learning about new digital tools and keeping abreast of changes in platform policies or relevant laws will empower individuals to make well-informed decisions regarding their digital legacies.

Digital Asset Policies

Creating comprehensive digital asset policies is a crucial step in securing your online legacy. As our lives become increasingly digitized, the assets we accrue online—ranging from social media accounts to cryptocurrency wallets—hold significant value and must be managed with care. Establishing a structured digital asset plan ensures that these assets are handled appropriately upon death, minimizing confusion among heirs and guaranteeing that your wishes are honored.

To begin developing a structured digital asset plan, it is essential to catalog all digital assets. This includes not only identifying each asset but also documenting access information such as usernames, passwords, and security questions. By maintaining an organized record, you create a single reference point for your heirs, reducing the chances of assets being overlooked or mismanaged. Additionally, consider specifying how each asset should be handled, whether it is to be transferred, deleted, or memorialized. This detailed approach can prevent potential disputes and ensure each asset is dealt with according to your preferences.

Understanding service agreements and their terms is another vital aspect of digital asset planning. Various online services have different policies regarding what happens to user accounts posthumously. For instance, some social media platforms offer options for memorializing accounts, while others may automatically delete them after a period of inactivity. Knowing these terms allows you to make informed decisions about how to manage your accounts. It's advisable to review the terms of service agreements for each platform where you hold an account and take note of any specific procedures or requirements for account management after death. This knowledge will enable your appointed representative to navigate the process smoothly without unnecessary delays or complications.

Incorporating guidelines into your plan is beneficial when dealing with service agreements. For each digital asset, provide clear instructions on actions to be taken based on the platform's policies. For example, if a social media account offers the option to memorialize, state whether this should be done and who is responsible for making the request. Detailed guidelines streamline the process, reduce ambiguities, and help ensure that your digital presence is handled in line with your wishes. These preparations can alleviate stress for your loved ones at an already difficult time.

Current laws surrounding digital asset inheritance add another layer of complexity to estate planning. Digital assets are often treated differently than physical assets, and legal frameworks governing their inheritance vary significantly by jurisdiction. It's crucial to stay informed about the applicable laws in your area, as these regulations dictate how digital assets are accessed, transferred, and taxed. Some states have enacted laws that give executors explicit authority to manage digital assets, while others require specific provisions to be included in wills or other estate planning documents to grant such authority. Consult with an estate planning attorney well-versed in digital asset law to ensure your plans comply with relevant legislation and that your digital assets are protected under the law.

Although current laws relating to digital asset inheritance do not necessitate specific guidelines, keeping abreast of legal developments is important for effective estate planning. Regulations are continually evolving to address new challenges posed by the digital age, and staying informed ensures that your plan remains compliant and up-to-date.

Clearly communicating your digital asset policies to family members is paramount for smooth transitions and setting expectations for all parties involved. Without clear communication, family members may be left uncertain about their roles and responsibilities, which can lead to confusion and conflict. It is advisable to discuss your digital asset plan with your chosen representatives and beneficiaries, ensuring they understand the location of the necessary documentation and the steps required to carry out your wishes.

Providing guidelines for communication can make a substantial difference. Establish a secure method for sharing sensitive information, such as passwords and security details, with your designated representatives. Consider using a digital vault or encrypted storage solution for this purpose. Additionally, outline the protocols for accessing this information and emphasize the importance of maintaining confidentiality to protect your digital assets from unauthorized access. These measures promote transparency and readiness, allowing your family to execute your plans efficiently.

Regularly revisiting your digital asset plan is equally important. As you acquire new digital assets or existing ones evolve, updating your record ensures no asset is left unaddressed. Conduct periodic reviews to confirm that your inventory is current and reflects any changes in ownership or value. Furthermore, verify that your specified guidelines for managing these assets remain appropriate and feasible. By keeping your digital asset plan dynamic, you adapt to changes in your digital life and maintain coherence in your overall estate strategy.

Incorporating into Wills and Trusts

Integrating digital assets into an existing estate plan is a crucial yet often overlooked aspect of legacy management. With the rise of online accounts, ranging from social media to cryptocurrency, it's essential to ensure that these assets are included in your estate plan to avoid potential disputes and confusion among heirs. This section will provide actionable steps for seamless integration, emphasizing the importance of clear definitions, regular updates, strategic asset planning, and involving heirs in the process.

First and foremost, using clear definitions and precise language when referencing digital assets in legal documents can prevent misinterpretation. Terms such as "digital assets" or "online accounts" should be explicitly defined within the context of your will or trust. For example, digital assets may include email accounts, social media profiles, online banking, investment accounts, and even cloud storage services. By clearly delineating what constitutes a digital asset, you minimize the risk of ambiguity and ensure that your intentions are accurately conveyed and executed.

It's also imperative to regularly update wills and trusts to include all evolving digital assets. The fast-paced nature of technology means that new types of digital assets are constantly emerging, and old ones may lose relevance. Regular reviews of your estate documents should be conducted to capture any changes in your digital footprint. This practice not only keeps your plans current but also helps avoid omissions that could lead to disputes among beneficiaries. For instance, if you acquire new digital currencies or subscribe to new online services, these should be promptly added to your will or trust.

Strategizing how digital assets fit into the larger estate portfolio is another key consideration. Digital assets should not be viewed in isolation; instead, they should be integrated into the overall estate plan to ensure coherence between digital and physical assets. This holistic approach helps set expectations for future heirs and aligns the distribution of both types of assets. For example, if you own significant digital art or NFTs, deciding how these will complement your physical art collection can provide a clearer picture for your heirs and ensure a balanced inheritance.

Engaging heirs in the estate planning process is equally important. Preparing them to manage digital assets responsibly involves educating them about the nature and value of these assets. This engagement can also cultivate a sense of duty regarding the family legacy. Involve your heirs early on by discussing your digital assets and explaining why you've chosen to distribute them in a particular way. For instance, if you have a valuable online business, explaining its operations and significance can prepare your heirs to either take over or manage the sale of the business after your passing.

Clear guidelines can help streamline this process for both you and your heirs. For example, providing instructions on how to access various accounts, passwords, and security measures will make it easier for your heirs to manage these assets without unnecessary complications. Utilizing digital tools like password managers or creating a secure document listing all relevant information can further simplify the process. Make sure this information is stored securely and shared with trusted individuals only.

Additionally, appointing a digital executor—someone specifically responsible for managing your digital assets—can provide clarity and efficiency in executing your digital asset wishes. This role is separate from your traditional executor and requires someone who understands the intricacies of digital property. A digital executor can handle tasks such as closing social media accounts, transferring digital assets, and ensuring compliance with service providers' terms of service.

Finally, consider the legal landscape surrounding digital assets, which varies by jurisdiction. Some regions have enacted laws that address the inheritance of digital assets, while others may not have specific regulations in place. Staying informed about local laws and seeking legal advice can help you navigate the complexities of incorporating digital assets into your estate plan. For example, the Revised Uniform Fiduciary Access to Digital Assets Act (RUFADAA) in the United States provides a framework for fiduciaries to manage digital assets, but implementation can differ from state to state.

Updating Your Digital Asset List

Regularly updating the list of digital assets is crucial to ensure comprehensive estate planning. As the digital landscape evolves rapidly, new platforms and types of digital assets continuously emerge, making it easy to forget or overlook updates. For instance, someone may have created a social media account on a new platform or invested in cryptocurrencies recently without documenting these in their estate plan. Such omissions can lead to significant challenges in managing and transferring these assets after their demise. Therefore, periodic reviews are essential to capture all changes and additions, ensuring that nothing slips through the cracks.

One must consider the rapid pace at which technology and digital assets evolve. New applications, investment opportunities, and digital storage methods are constantly developed, each potentially holding value. A person might engage in online gaming and acquire valuable in-game items or start an online business that becomes profitable. Without regular updates, these assets could be overlooked. Periodic reviews help individuals remain aware of what they possess digitally, preventing any assets from being lost or forgotten.

Regularly updated lists also prevent lost opportunities for asset transfer by accounting for changes in digital asset ownership. Digital assets can change hands or ownership status quickly. For instance, selling an online business or transferring domain names should be reflected in the estate plan. If such transactions are not documented, it could result in complications during the asset transfer process. By maintaining an up-to-date list, the current state of ownership is clearly documented, facilitating smoother transitions for heirs and beneficiaries.

Organized records of digital assets play a crucial role in their management and access for appointed individuals. When individuals pass away or become incapacitated, appointed executors or trustees need to manage and distribute these assets as per the deceased's wishes. If the records are disorganized or incomplete, it becomes challenging for them to locate and identify all digital assets. Clear documentation, including login credentials, account details, and specific instructions, ensures that these individuals can efficiently manage the assets without unnecessary delays or confusion. This organization not only alleviates stress for the appointed individuals but also ensures that the assets are handled according to the original owner's intentions.

Routine audits of digital assets help maintain an up-to-date inventory for accurate estate planning. Just as one conducts financial audits to ensure proper management of physical assets, digital assets require similar attention. Conducting regular audits helps identify any discrepancies, ensures that no asset is left unaccounted for, and verifies that all information is current. This practice is particularly important given the intangible nature of digital assets, which can easily be modified, transferred, or deleted. Regular audits create a habit of vigilance, reinforcing the importance of keeping the digital estate plan as accurate and comprehensive as possible.

In terms of guidelines for conducting these updates and reviews, it's advisable to set a routine schedule. Depending on the volume and complexity of one's digital assets, this could be bi-annual or annual. During these scheduled reviews, individuals should take stock of all new assets acquired within the period, any changes in existing assets, and ensure that all login credentials and necessary information are up-to-date. It's also beneficial to involve trusted advisors or legal professionals in this process. They can provide insights into any legal implications of new digital assets and offer guidance on properly documenting these assets in the estate plan.

Another practical guideline involves creating a master document or digital vault where all digital assets and their corresponding details are stored securely. This document should include information like usernames, passwords, security question answers, and specific instructions for handling each asset. The digital vault should be accessible only to designated individuals to prevent unauthorized access while ensuring that the right people can manage the assets when necessary.

Including detailed instructions on how to access and manage the digital assets can greatly aid appointed individuals. These instructions should cover all potential scenarios, such as how to handle social media accounts, online banking details, cryptocurrency wallets, and other valuable digital assets. Providing clear, step-by-step guidance ensures that there is no ambiguity during the execution of the estate plan.

Furthermore, staying informed about changes in digital asset regulations and platform policies is essential. Digital platforms frequently update their terms of service, which can impact how assets are accessed or managed posthumously. Regularly reviewing these terms and adjusting the estate plan accordingly can prevent legal complications in the future.

Lastly, communicating the importance of digital asset management to family members and beneficiaries can foster a collaborative approach to estate planning. By educating them on the significance of digital assets and the necessity of regular updates, individuals can ensure that their loved ones understand the process and are prepared to assist if needed. This communication also helps in setting clear expectations and reducing potential conflicts among beneficiaries.

Understanding and managing digital assets is crucial for thorough estate planning. This chapter has delved into identifying the various types of digital assets, such as social media accounts, cryptocurrencies, and online banking credentials, helping readers recognize their importance in legacy management. By categorizing these assets into personal, financial, and professional sections, individuals can better organize and protect them. Valuing these assets accurately and documenting them with clear instructions ensures they are handled according to one's wishes and minimizes conflicts among heirs.

Access and control issues surrounding digital assets were also discussed, highlighting the need to understand different platform policies and privacy laws. Proactively designating trusted persons to manage these assets can prevent legal disputes and unauthorized access. Utilizing technological tools, such as digital vaults, can safeguard sensitive information and simplify the transfer process. Continuous education about evolving technologies and legal requirements empowers individuals to make informed decisions, ensuring their digital legacies are effectively managed and protected for future generations.

CHAPTER 11

International Estate Planning

Managing international assets and beneficiaries involves navigating a maze of legal complexities, often requiring a nuanced understanding of varying jurisdictions. As individuals acquire properties or investments in multiple countries, they are faced with distinct legal frameworks that can significantly influence how their estates are administered. These differences extend beyond mere paperwork; they can affect who has the right to manage the estate, how assets are divided among heirs, and the tax implications that arise from cross-border holdings.

In this chapter, we will explore the intricacies of cross-border estate planning, focusing on jurisdictional challenges and the impact of differing inheritance laws. We will discuss practical strategies such as consulting with international legal experts to ensure compliance with local regulations, as well as the benefits of alternative structures like foundations when traditional trusts are not recognized. Additionally, we will cover methods of resolving disputes through mediation and arbitration to avoid lengthy and costly court battles. By the end of this chapter, readers will gain a comprehensive understanding of how to navigate the legal landscape to protect and effectively manage their international estates.

Cross-border Legal Considerations

In the realm of estate planning, navigating the complexities of managing assets across different countries can feel like traversing a labyrinth. It's critical to understand how varying jurisdictions influence estate administration and what measures one can take to safeguard their global assets effectively.

Firstly, let's examine how different jurisdictions can impact estate administration. The geographical location of your assets significantly dictates which legal framework will govern them. For instance, if you own property in both the United States and France, each country has its own set of rules that must be followed. These laws are known as "jurisdictional" because they provide guidelines on who has the authority to administer these estates. Understanding jurisdictional issues is paramount, as failing to adhere to a country's specific regulations can lead to significant delays, additional costs, or even loss of control over assets.

One practical way to mitigate jurisdictional challenges is by consulting with international legal experts familiar with the estate laws of all relevant countries. These professionals can offer tailored guidance on structuring your estate plan in a manner that complies with diverse legal requirements while ensuring a smooth administration process.

Next, we delve into the variability in inheritance laws across different nations. Inheritance laws—sometimes referred to as succession laws—govern the distribution of an individual's estate following their death. These rules can vary drastically from one country to another, potentially impacting who inherits what portion of your estate. In countries like the United Kingdom, for example, the principle of "freedom of testamentary disposition" typically permits individuals considerable liberty in choosing their heirs. In contrast, French law mandates a reserved portion of the estate must go to the deceased's children, regardless of any conflicting wishes expressed in a will.

Understanding how these differences could affect your estate's distribution is crucial. If your estate plan does not take these variances into account, the outcomes might contradict your intentions, potentially leading to family disputes and litigation. Additionally, some countries have community property laws that can significantly impact asset division upon death. Married couples should be particularly cautious, as owning property in a community property jurisdiction may mean that your spouse automatically owns half of certain assets, regardless of what your will states.

Moving on to how U.S. trusts are treated abroad, it's important to note that not all countries recognize the concept of a trust. In the United States, living trusts are common tools for managing and protecting assets during one's lifetime and facilitating easier transfer upon death. However, countries such as Germany and France do not recognize these trusts, complicating asset management for international estates. This non-recognition can create difficulties in enforcing the terms of the trust, leading to administrative challenges and unintended tax consequences.

To navigate these obstacles, it can be beneficial to establish alternative structures, such as foundations or other legal entities recognized internationally. Moreover, thorough documentation and clear communication with beneficiaries and foreign executors can help ensure that the intended management and distribution of trust assets are honored, despite jurisdictional differences. Legal advice from professionals knowledgeable in cross-border estate planning is invaluable in this context.

Lastly, resolving international estate disputes often requires specialized approaches. Mediation and arbitration are two methods that can be employed to address conflicts without resorting to lengthy and costly court battles. Mediation involves a neutral third-party mediator who assists the disputing parties in reaching a mutually satisfactory agreement. This approach can save time and resources, preserve family relationships, and maintain privacy, which is often lost in public court proceedings.

Arbitration, on the other hand, involves an arbitrator or panel of arbitrators who render a decision after hearing both sides' arguments. While more formal than mediation, arbitration is still generally quicker and less expensive than traditional litigation. It offers a binding resolution to the dispute and can be particularly useful in cases where parties are located in different countries, providing a streamlined process for enforcement in multiple jurisdictions.

Awareness of local dispute resolution procedures can further minimize delays in asset distribution. International conventions, such as the Hague Convention on the Recognition and Enforcement of Foreign Judgments, play a crucial role in ensuring that arbitration awards and mediated agreements are respected and enforced across borders.

Tax Treaties

Understanding how tax treaties between countries can aid in minimizing double taxation on estates with international ties is critical for effective estate planning. This subpoint delves into the mechanisms through which such treaties operate, providing insight into their application and potential benefits.

First, identifying relevant tax treaties applicable to your estate planning is essential. Tax treaties are agreements between two or more countries that set standards for tax-related matters, including the handling of estates. These treaties often include provisions to prevent double taxation, where the same asset is taxed by multiple jurisdictions. To begin, one must determine the jurisdictions involved in their estate planning—the countries where assets are held and where beneficiaries reside. Once these jurisdictions are identified, you can then research any existing tax treaties between these countries. It's important to consult legal databases, government websites, or work with a legal professional specializing in international tax law to ensure that all relevant treaties are considered.

When exploring applicable tax treaties, it's crucial to understand the specific clauses related to estate taxes. Many treaties include articles that outline how estates will be taxed, ensuring that only one country applies estate taxes. For instance, if an individual has properties in both the United States and France, the US-France tax treaty provides provisions to mitigate double taxation, specifying how each country will tax the estate and where credits can be claimed.

Next, we move on to calculating possible tax implications on estate assets internationally. This process involves assessing the value of estate assets in each jurisdiction and applying the respective country's tax laws. Let's take an example to illustrate this: Suppose you own properties in three different countries. Each country has its own method of valuing property and its own estate tax rate. The first step is to have each property appraised according to local standards. Once you've established the value, you will then apply the local estate tax rate to determine the initial tax liability in each country.

Beyond mere calculations, understanding the nuances of tax laws in each country is paramount. Some countries might offer exemptions for certain types of assets or for smaller estate values, while others impose stringent taxes regardless of the estate's size. Engaging with tax professionals who are well-versed in international law can help navigate these complexities, ensuring that all potential savings are realized.

Now, let's discuss the diversity in taxation on inheritances and gifts across different countries. Every nation has distinct rules about how inheritances and gifts are taxed, which can significantly affect your estate plan. For instance, in the United Kingdom, inheritance tax is charged based on the value of the deceased person's estate over a certain threshold, whereas in Germany, both the relationship to the deceased and the size of the inheritance determine the tax rate. Similarly, the United States imposes federal estate tax but allows a considerable exemption amount, reducing the number of estates subject to taxation.

It's essential to take these differences into account when planning your estate. For example, if you wish to leave a substantial gift to a beneficiary in another country, you should research that country's gift tax regulations. Some may exclude gifts from taxation if they fall below a specified limit, while others might levy substantial taxes even on moderate gifts. Understanding these distinctions ensures that beneficiaries receive the intended amount without being unduly burdened by taxes.

Finally, we address how to claim credits to offset estate taxes, leading to substantial savings. Most tax treaties include provisions allowing taxpayers to claim credits for taxes paid in another country. These credits effectively reduce the total tax burden, as they offset the amount owed in the taxpayer's home country by the amount already paid abroad.

To claim these credits, one typically needs to gather documentation proving the payment of foreign estate taxes. This might include tax receipts, payment confirmations, and official correspondence from the foreign tax authority. Once collected, these documents are submitted to the tax authorities in the taxpayer's home country along with their estate tax return. It's important to keep meticulous records, as tax authorities often require detailed evidence to approve claims.

Let's illustrate with an example. Suppose you have an estate subject to taxes in both Canada and Italy. You would first pay the necessary estate taxes in Italy. Once the Italian tax is settled, you compile the documented proof of this payment and submit it with your Canadian tax return. The Canadian tax authorities will then credit the amount paid in Italy against your total Canadian estate tax liability, ensuring you aren't taxed twice on the same assets.

Foreign Trusts

Considering the complexities of international estate planning, establishing foreign trusts often emerges as a crucial strategy. This subpoint discusses the implications and effectiveness of such trusts in managing cross-border assets and ensuring the protection of beneficiaries.

Understanding Foreign Trust Regulations

Understanding critical differences in trust laws globally is essential to the creation and management of foreign trusts. Each country has its own framework governing how trusts can be established and operated. For example, common law countries like the UK and Australia have well-established trust legislation that might differ significantly from civil law countries where trust concepts may not even exist. These variations can affect everything from the selection of trustees to the administration of the trust.

It's essential, therefore, to consult with legal experts familiar with the jurisdiction in question. In some regions, rigid regulations may restrict who can serve as a trustee or dictate specific uses for trust assets. Many countries also impose stringent disclosure requirements, which could pose privacy concerns for those looking to maintain confidentiality around their estate plans. When structuring a foreign trust, understanding these regulatory nuances helps ensure compliance and avoids potential pitfalls.

Moreover, knowing the residence status of both trustees and beneficiaries is vital. Some jurisdictions may consider the trust domestic if most of the administrative actions occur within their borders, subjecting it to local laws and taxes. Properly navigating these distinctions can be the difference between a successful international estate plan and a complex legal quagmire.

Strategic Advantages of Foreign Trusts

Using foreign trusts comes with various strategic advantages, particularly in terms of asset protection and tax benefits. One notable benefit is shielding assets from creditors. Placing assets in a foreign trust makes it more challenging for domestic creditors to access them due to jurisdictional barriers. This form of asset protection is especially valuable in contentious situations like divorce proceedings or business insolvency.

Foreign trusts also present favorable tax implications. Some countries offer advantageous tax rates or exemptions on income generated by trust assets. Selecting a jurisdiction known for its tax benefits can result in significant savings, thus enhancing the overall value of the estate. However, it's crucial to remember that improper handling of trust assets or failure to comply with local laws can negate these benefits, making expert advice indispensable.

An additional advantage lies in the ability to diversify investments across international markets, potentially yielding higher returns. By broadening the investment scope, trustees can position the trust for growth while mitigating risks associated with investing solely in one country's market. This diversification can be particularly beneficial in volatile economic periods, providing a buffer against market downturns.

Maintenance and Administration Challenges

While foreign trusts can provide significant advantages, they come with ongoing responsibilities, including compliance with both U.S. and foreign regulations. Maintaining proper documentation is one such responsibility. Both the United States and the foreign jurisdiction will likely require detailed records of transactions involving the trust. Failure to maintain accurate records can result in fines or penalties, complicating the management of the trust.

Regular reporting to tax authorities is another critical element. Trustees must file annual returns detailing income, expenses, and distributions. Inaccurate or incomplete filings can attract scrutiny from tax authorities, leading to audits and possible legal action. This requirement underscores the importance of having a proficient accountant familiar with international tax law involved in the trust's administration.

Furthermore, trustees must remain vigilant about changes in legislation. Laws governing trusts can evolve, altering regulatory requirements and impacting the trust's operation. Regular consultations with legal professionals ensure that the trust remains compliant, preventing costly legal complications.

Additionally, communication between trustees and beneficiaries requires careful management. Differences in time zones and communication preferences can complicate interactions, necessitating clear, documented processes for regular updates. Establishing these protocols early enhances transparency and fosters trust among parties involved.

Tax Implications of Foreign Trusts

The taxation of foreign trusts involves several layers of complexity, both in the U.S. and abroad. In the United States, foreign trusts are generally treated according to the status of the settlor and the beneficiaries. If the settlor or any beneficiary is a U.S. person, the trust might be subject to additional reporting requirements, including the infamous Form 3520 and Form 3520-A. Noncompliance can result in substantial penalties, emphasizing the need for meticulous attention to detail.

Abroad, the tax treatment of foreign trusts varies widely. Some countries may impose taxes on income generated within their borders, while others might exempt certain types of income altogether. Identifying a jurisdiction with favorable tax treaties can minimize the risk of double taxation—where the same income is taxed in two different countries. Utilizing these treaties requires precise knowledge and navigation, often requiring specialized legal and tax expertise.

Navigating these intricacies is not without challenges. Double taxation can still occur despite efforts to mitigate it, primarily because tax treaties do not cover every possible scenario. Moreover, differing definitions of what constitutes taxable income or deductible expenses can further complicate filings. Setting up a strategy to handle these tricky aspects ahead of time can save considerable time and money down the road.

Dealing with Different Jurisdictions

Understanding Estate Jurisdictions

Navigating international estate planning requires a comprehensive understanding of the various jurisdictions that might affect your estate. Each country has its own laws and regulations regarding property, inheritance, taxes, and more. To begin with, it is essential to identify all the jurisdictions involved—this could include countries where you own property, hold bank accounts, or have beneficiaries residing.

For example, if you own a vacation home in France, investments in Canada, and have children living in Japan, each of these jurisdictions will have specific laws impacting your estate. In France, for instance, there are strict forced heirship rules dictating how property must be distributed among heirs. Canada has tax implications for non-resident investors, and Japan may impose different rules on foreign inheritances. Being aware of these differences helps prevent unexpected complications and ensures compliance with local laws.

Consulting Professionals for Multi-Jurisdictional Guidance

Due to the complexity of managing an international estate, seeking guidance from professionals experienced in multiple legal systems is invaluable. An estate planning attorney with international expertise can help navigate the differing rules and regulations. Likewise, a financial advisor knowledgeable about cross-border tax strategies can provide advice tailored to your unique situation.

When choosing professionals, ensure they have a solid understanding of applicable laws in all relevant jurisdictions. For instance, an attorney specializing in U.S. law might not fully comprehend the nuances of German inheritance taxes. Engaging a network of professionals who can collaborate effectively ensures that your estate plan is cohesive and compliant globally. Collaborative efforts between attorneys, accountants, and financial advisors across jurisdictions result in a well-rounded strategy, minimizing legal risks and maximizing asset protection.

Harmonizing Estate Documents Across Jurisdictions

One critical aspect of international estate planning involves harmonizing estate documents across multiple jurisdictions. This means ensuring that wills, trusts, and other legal documents are recognized and enforceable in all relevant countries. Discrepancies between documents in different jurisdictions can lead to legal disputes and delays in asset distribution.

For example, having a will drafted in the United States might not automatically be recognized in Spain without proper validation. To avoid such issues, consider creating distinct estate plans in each jurisdiction while maintaining consistency in the overall directives. Including choice-of-law clauses specifying which country's laws govern the estate can reduce conflicts among beneficiaries.

In practice, one might create a separate will for assets located in each jurisdiction but ensure that each document aligns with the overarching estate plan. Keeping detailed records and clear instructions helps executors and trustees manage the estate efficiently.

Guideline: Consult with legal experts in each jurisdiction to verify that estate documents comply with local laws. Periodic reviews of these documents with international professionals ensure they remain up-to-date with changing laws.

Adapting Estate Plans to Jurisdictional Changes

Estate laws and regulations can change, requiring periodic adjustments to your estate plan. Staying abreast of legal modifications in relevant jurisdictions is crucial to maintain compliance and protect your assets. This includes understanding when and how to update your estate plan to reflect changes in property laws, tax codes, and inheritance rules.

For example, if a country where you own property introduces new inheritance tax laws, it may necessitate revisions to your estate plan to mitigate tax liabilities. Similarly, changes in family circumstances like marriage, divorce, or acquiring new assets also warrant updates to ensure the estate plan remains effective.

Regular consultation with your team of international professionals can provide insights into potential impacts of legal changes. They can recommend timely updates and strategic modifications needed to adapt to evolving laws. Implementing a system for periodic reviews and adjustments stabilizes your estate plan, reflecting current legal landscapes.

Guideline: Schedule regular reviews of your estate plan with legal and financial professionals. Update documents as needed to align with any changes in the law or personal circumstances, ensuring ongoing compliance and asset protection.

Conclusion

Managing an estate that spans multiple jurisdictions presents unique challenges, but with careful planning and professional guidance, it is feasible to create a robust, compliant estate plan. Start by understanding the relevant jurisdictions and their legal requirements. Engage knowledgeable professionals to navigate complexities and harmonize estate documents across borders. Stay proactive in adapting your estate plan to changes, ensuring your assets are protected and your intentions fulfilled.

Dispute Resolution Mechanisms

Resolving international estate disputes efficiently is a critical aspect of managing cross-border assets and ensuring that beneficiaries receive their inheritances without unnecessary delay or expense. This subpoint explores the various methods available to achieve such resolutions, focusing on mediation and arbitration, legal strategies, local dispute resolution awareness, and jurisdictional complexities.

Mediation and arbitration are two effective routes for preventing protracted court battles when it comes to international estate disputes. Mediation involves a neutral third-party mediator who facilitates dialogue between disputing parties to help them reach a mutually agreeable solution. It is particularly beneficial in maintaining relationships among heirs and preserving family harmony, as it allows for more personalized and confidential negotiations. Arbitration, on the other hand, involves an arbitrator who listens to both sides' arguments and makes a binding decision. While it can be more formal than mediation, arbitration still offers a quicker, less publicized, and often less costly alternative to litigation. Both methods emphasize resolving conflicts outside of traditional courts, thereby saving time and financial resources for all involved parties.

A proper legal strategy is paramount in ensuring efficient resolutions of international estate disputes. This involves several key elements including clear communication, thorough documentation, and proactive legal counseling. Engaging attorneys with expertise in international estate law can help in drafting documents that anticipate potential conflicts and include dispute resolution clauses. These clauses can specify preferred methods like mediation or arbitration, detailing how and where disputes should be resolved if they arise. Additionally, having a well-defined plan that aligns with the estate holder's wishes and local laws reduces the likelihood of misunderstandings that could lead to disputes. Careful planning also includes regular updates to the estate plan to reflect any changes in personal circumstances or international laws.

Another crucial element is the awareness of local dispute resolution procedures, which can significantly minimize delays in asset distribution. Each country has its own set of rules and protocols for handling estate disputes, and being familiar with these can streamline the resolution process. For instance, the processes for mediating disputes in European countries may differ from those in Asian jurisdictions. Estate planners and executors must be aware of these differences to ensure that they are acting within the legal frameworks of the respective countries. This knowledge helps in navigating the legal landscape effectively and avoiding procedural missteps that could result in prolonged settlement periods.

Misunderstanding jurisdictional matters can have far-reaching implications, potentially leading to unintended distribution outcomes. Jurisdictional issues arise when there is ambiguity over which country's laws should apply to specific aspects of the estate. Factors such as the domicile of the deceased, the location of assets, and the residency of beneficiaries can complicate these matters. For example, an estate comprised of properties in multiple countries may be subject to different inheritance laws, leading to conflicts about which legal standards apply. If not properly addressed, this confusion can result in conflicting judgments from different jurisdictions, thereby delaying or complicating the distribution of assets. To mitigate these risks, it is vital to seek guidance from legal professionals who specialize in multi-jurisdictional estate planning. They can provide insights into which laws will govern the estate's assets and suggest strategies to harmonize the distribution process.

Navigating the complexities of managing international assets and beneficiaries requires careful consideration and informed decision-making. This chapter has explored key legal considerations that impact estate administration across borders, including jurisdictional issues, inheritance laws, and the recognition of trusts. Understanding these factors is essential for developing a robust estate plan that complies with diverse legal frameworks and ensures the smooth transfer of assets. By consulting with international legal experts and adopting tailored strategies, individuals can mitigate potential challenges and secure their global assets effectively.

Furthermore, this chapter highlighted the importance of awareness regarding tax treaties, foreign trust regulations, and dispute resolution mechanisms. Tax treaties play a vital role in minimizing double taxation, while understanding foreign trust laws can offer significant advantages in asset protection and tax benefits. Additionally, employing mediation and arbitration can resolve disputes efficiently, preserving family relationships and avoiding prolonged legal battles. By integrating these insights into their estate planning, readers can confidently manage cross-border assets and safeguard their beneficiaries' interests.

CHAPTER 12

Charitable Giving Strategies

Charitable giving offers a unique way to integrate philanthropy into your estate planning, ensuring that your financial goals align with the causes you care about most. By employing charitable giving strategies, you can create a lasting legacy while making a meaningful impact. This chapter delves into how different planned giving options can help you achieve these objectives.

Throughout this chapter, you will explore various types of planned gifts, such as bequests, retirement accounts, donor-advised funds (DAFs), and charitable remainder trusts (CRTs). Each option comes with its own set of benefits and characteristics tailored to fit different financial situations and philanthropic goals. The discussion also covers practical advice on incorporating charitable bequests into wills, the flexibility offered by DAFs, and the dual benefits provided by CRTs, including both financial returns and philanthropic contributions. Additionally, the chapter provides insights into setting up charitable trusts, choosing beneficiaries, and complying with legal requirements to ensure that your charitable intentions are fully realized.

Planned Giving Options

Exploring different planned giving options can help you create a lasting impact through your estate plan. Understanding these choices not only aligns your financial goals with meaningful contributions but also offers various benefits to both you and the charitable organizations you support.

Types of Planned Gifts include bequests, retirement accounts, donor-advised funds (DAFs), and charitable remainder trusts (CRTs). Each option has unique characteristics and advantages that can cater to different financial situations and philanthropic intentions.

Types of Planned Gifts

One of the most common forms of planned giving is the bequest. Bequests are provisions in a will or trust that allocate assets to a designated charity upon your passing. They are flexible since you can modify them as your circumstances change. The simplicity of bequests makes them an excellent starting point for those new to estate planning.

Retirement accounts also offer a straightforward mechanism for planned giving. By naming a charitable organization as a beneficiary of your retirement account, you ensure that the remaining funds go directly to your chosen cause. This method avoids probate, making it an efficient way to contribute. Additionally, because charities do not pay income tax on the gifts they receive, this type of donation can be more beneficial compared to leaving retirement assets to heirs, who would be subject to taxes.

Donor-Advised Funds (DAFs) are another flexible option. A DAF is an individual charitable account maintained by a sponsoring organization, which allows you to make a tax-deductible donation, then recommend grants to charities over time. This setup provides ongoing engagement and the opportunity to involve family members in philanthropic activities, fostering a tradition of giving across generations. Moreover, DAFs can be particularly advantageous during years of high income since contributions provide immediate tax deductions while allowing you to decide later which charities will receive your support.

Charitable Remainder Trusts (CRTs) offer dual benefits: they provide you with an income stream during your lifetime and leave the remaining assets to charity after you pass away. CRTs are irrevocable trusts that can sell appreciated assets without incurring capital gains taxes, reinvest the proceeds, and distribute income to you or your designated beneficiaries. The process generates an immediate charitable income tax deduction, based on the present value of the future gift to charity. This mechanism makes CRTs an attractive option for individuals seeking both financial and philanthropic returns.

Bequests in Wills

Incorporating charitable bequests into your will is relatively simple but requires careful planning to ensure your intentions are fully realized. Begin by clearly identifying the specific charities you wish to support in your will, using precise language to avoid any confusion or misinterpretation. You can choose between several types of bequests: a specific dollar amount, a percentage of your estate, or particular assets such as stocks or real estate.

A helpful strategy is to coordinate with both your legal advisor and the charitable organizations to ensure your bequest complies with their donation acceptance policies. Some charities may have specific requirements or restrictions regarding the types of assets they accept or how donations must be structured. By engaging with the charities beforehand, you can align your bequest with their needs and maximize its impact.

Another option is to create a contingent bequest, which designates an alternate beneficiary if the primary charity cannot accept the gift. This flexibility ensures that your philanthropic goals remain intact, even if unforeseen circumstances arise. To maintain the relevance of your charitable bequests, periodically review and update your will as needed, especially following significant life events like marriage, divorce, or acquiring substantial new assets.

Donor-Advised Funds (DAFs)

DAFs serve as versatile instruments for charitable giving. When you establish a DAF, you donate assets—such as cash, securities, or other property—to the fund, managed by a public charity. These contributions are eligible for an immediate tax deduction, but the funds can be distributed to charities over many years, providing a prolonged engagement with your philanthropy.

One of the primary advantages of DAFs is the ability to invest the donated assets, potentially growing the fund's value and increasing the overall impact of your contributions. Many DAF providers offer various investment options tailored to your risk tolerance and financial goals, allowing you to balance growth and security.

DAFs also simplify record-keeping and grant management, as the sponsoring organization handles administrative tasks like issuing checks to charitable recipients and maintaining detailed records of donations and grants. This convenience is particularly appealing for individuals who wish to focus more on their philanthropic vision rather than the administrative intricacies.

Additionally, DAFs can play a critical role in involving family members in charitable decision-making. By establishing a DAF, you can designate successors or advisors to continue recommending grants, creating a legacy of giving that span generations. This collaborative approach encourages family discussions about values and priorities, fostering a shared commitment to philanthropy.

Charitable Remainder Trusts (CRTs)

CRTs are powerful tools for individuals looking to integrate charitable giving with financial planning. Establishing a CRT involves transferring assets into an irrevocable trust, which then pays you or designated beneficiaries an income stream for a specified period or for life. Upon termination of the trust, the remaining assets go to the named charity.

Two main types of CRTs exist: charitable remainder annuity trusts (CRATs) and charitable remainder unitrusts (CRUTs). CRATs pay a fixed annual amount, providing predictable income regardless of the trust's investment performance. In contrast, CRUTs pay a variable amount based on a percentage of the trust's value, adjusting with the trust's investment returns. Choosing between a CRAT and CRUT depends on your financial needs and risk tolerance.

The income generated by CRTs can be particularly beneficial if you have highly appreciated assets, such as stocks or real estate. By donating these assets to a CRT, you avoid capital gains taxes, effectively converting them into a diversified portfolio that produces income. This tax advantage enhances the appeal of CRTs as a financial strategy, while the immediate charitable income tax deduction incentivizes their use in estate planning.

Setting Up Charitable Trusts

Establishing Charitable Trusts

Incorporating charitable trusts into an estate plan is a highly effective strategy for individuals looking to combine their philanthropic goals with financial planning. Establishing a charitable trust involves several important steps, each requiring careful consideration to ensure the trust fulfills its intended purpose.

First and foremost, it's essential to consult with legal and financial advisors who specialize in estate planning and charitable giving. These experts can guide you through the legal intricacies, ensuring that the formation of the trust complies with all applicable laws and regulations.

The initial step in creating a charitable trust is to determine your philanthropic objectives. This involves identifying the types of causes or organizations you wish to support. Once you have a clear vision, you'll need to draft a trust document, outlining the specific terms and provisions. This document should include details such as the assets to be placed in the trust, the distribution method, and the duration of the trust.

Next, the trust must be funded. This involves transferring the designated assets into the trust. Assets can include cash, securities, real estate, or other valuable property. It's crucial to ensure that the transfer process is properly documented and adheres to the stipulations outlined in the trust document.

Administration is another key aspect of establishing a charitable trust. Trustees must be appointed to manage the trust's assets and ensure compliance with the established terms. Choosing trustees requires careful consideration; they should possess the expertise and dedication needed to fulfill their fiduciary duties effectively.

Types of Charitable Trusts

Charitable trusts come in various forms, each serving different purposes and offering unique benefits. Two of the most commonly used trusts are Charitable Lead Trusts (CLTs) and Charitable Remainder Trusts (CRTs).

A Charitable Lead Trust (CLT) provides immediate benefits to a chosen charity by allowing the organization to receive income from the trust for a specified period. Once this period ends, the remaining assets revert to the donor or the donor's beneficiaries. CLTs offer significant tax advantages, including potential deductions on gift and estate taxes.

On the other hand, a Charitable Remainder Trust (CRT) provides income to the donor or other non-charitable beneficiaries for life or a specified term of years. Afterward, the remaining assets are transferred to the designated charity. CRTs can be particularly beneficial for individuals seeking to generate a steady income stream while ultimately supporting a charitable cause. Additionally, CRTs offer the potential for income tax deductions based on the present value of the remainder interest that will eventually go to charity.

Choosing Beneficiaries

Selecting the right beneficiaries is a critical step in establishing a charitable trust. This process should align closely with your personal values and philanthropic goals. Start by identifying the causes or issues that matter most to you. Whether it's education, healthcare, environmental conservation, or social justice, choosing a focus area will help narrow down potential beneficiaries.

Once you've identified your focus, research organizations within that field. Look for reputable charities with a proven track record of effective use of funds and positive impact. Online resources, charity watchdog groups, and recommendations from trusted advisors can be valuable tools in this process.

It's also essential to consider the long-term sustainability of the chosen organizations. Ensure they have sound governance structures, financial stability, and a clear mission that aligns with your values. Determining how the contributions will be used is equally important. Some donors prefer unrestricted donations, giving the charity flexibility to allocate funds where needed most, while others choose to support specific programs or projects.

Once you've selected potential beneficiaries, reach out to them directly. Engaging in conversations with representatives from these organizations can provide deeper insights into their operations, goals, and how they plan to utilize the contributions. This direct interaction can also establish a personal connection and foster a greater sense of involvement in their work.

Compliance and Maintenance

Ongoing compliance and maintenance are essential for the successful operation of a charitable trust. Trustees play a vital role in ensuring that the trust adheres to all rules and regulations governing charitable trusts, maintaining accurate records, and fulfilling reporting requirements.

One of the primary responsibilities of trustees is to ensure that the trust operates in accordance with the terms outlined in the trust document. This includes managing the assets prudently, making distributions as specified, and maintaining transparency in all transactions. Regular audits and reviews can help identify any discrepancies and ensure compliance with legal requirements.

Accurate record-keeping is crucial for both legal compliance and effective management of the trust. Detailed records of all transactions, asset valuations, income distributions, and expenses should be maintained meticulously. These records not only facilitate transparency but also serve as essential documentation for tax reporting and audits.

Tax compliance is another critical aspect of managing a charitable trust. Trustees must ensure that the trust meets all federal and state tax obligations. This includes filing annual tax returns, adhering to charitable contribution substantiation requirements, and staying informed about any changes in tax laws that may affect the trust.

Furthermore, trustees should regularly communicate with the beneficiaries to keep them informed about the trust's activities, financial status, and future plans. Transparent communication fosters trust and ensures alignment between the donor's intentions and the organization's actions.

Periodic reviews of the trust's performance and effectiveness can help identify areas for improvement and ensure that the trust continues to fulfill its charitable mission. Trustees may also need to adapt the trust's strategies in response to changing circumstances, such as shifts in the donor's financial situation, modifications in tax laws, or evolving needs of the beneficiaries.

Tax Advantages of Charitable Contributions

Charitable giving can provide significant tax benefits, ensuring that your contributions not only support the causes you care about but also enhance your financial well-being. Understanding these advantages allows you to maximize both your philanthropic impact and savings.

Income tax deductions are a primary benefit of charitable giving. When you donate to qualified charities, you can deduct the amount from your taxable income, thus lowering your overall tax bill. For instance, if you are in the 24% tax bracket and make a $1,000 donation, you could potentially reduce your tax liability by $240. To claim these deductions, it's crucial to maintain proper documentation. Ensure you have receipts for all donations, noting the date, charity name, and donation amount. For donations over $250, the IRS requires a written acknowledgment from the charity, specifying whether any goods or services were received in exchange for the gift.

Another substantial benefit arises in the form of estate tax reductions through charitable giving. By including charitable bequests in your will, you can lower the value of your taxable estate. This means a smaller portion of your assets will be subject to estate taxes, which can significantly reduce the tax burden on your heirs. There are strategic ways to leverage this benefit, such as making lifetime gifts, which not only reduce your estate's taxable value but also may qualify for income tax deductions. Consulting with an estate planning attorney can provide guidance on integrating these strategies effectively into your overall plan.

Tax-free transfers to charities offer another avenue for maximizing tax efficiency. Certain gifts, like appreciated securities, can be transferred to charities without incurring capital gains taxes. For example, if you own stock that has significantly increased in value, donating the stock directly to a charity rather than selling it first can avoid the capital gains tax while still providing a deduction for the full market value of the stock. This method is particularly beneficial for high-net-worth individuals looking to minimize tax exposure while supporting charitable endeavors.

Utilizing trusts, such as Charitable Remainder Trusts (CRTs) and Charitable Lead Trusts (CLTs), can also facilitate tax savings. A CRT allows you to receive an income stream for a specified period or life, after which the remaining assets go to the designated charity. This setup provides immediate income tax deductions, reduces estate taxes, and can help diversify and manage investment risk within the trust. Conversely, a CLT involves the charity receiving income from the trust for a set term, with the remaining assets eventually going to your beneficiaries. Both these options can be complex, so involving tax professionals is critical to navigate the legalities and optimize the benefits effectively.

For example, consider creating a Charitable Remainder Unitrust (CRUT), where the donor receives a variable annual payout based on a percentage of the trust's assets. The flexibility of CRUTs often makes them attractive, as they adjust payouts according to the trust's performance, aligning with market conditions. On the other hand, Charitable Remainder Annuity Trusts (CRATs) provide fixed annual payments, offering stability regardless of market fluctuations. Each type serves different financial goals, and a financial advisor can help determine the most suitable option.

Properly utilizing these charitable giving strategies ensures that your contributions make a meaningful impact while simultaneously providing substantial tax benefits. Careful planning and adherence to tax regulations are essential, and professional advice can make the process smoother and more effective. Through these methods, you can create a legacy that reflects your values and supports future generations.

It's important to stay updated on tax laws, as policies and limits on deductions can change. Regular consultations with tax advisors will keep you informed and ensure compliance with current legislation. Moreover, they can assist in documenting your contributions accurately, an essential aspect of claiming all available tax benefits.

Creating a Family Foundation

A family foundation can be an effective way to integrate philanthropy into your estate planning, allowing you to build a lasting legacy and contribute meaningfully to causes that are important to you. However, understanding the basics of family foundations, their structure, and how to establish one is crucial before embarking on this journey.

One common point of confusion is the difference between a family foundation and a charitable trust. Though both aim to support charitable activities, they differ significantly in structure and operation. A family foundation is typically a private entity established by an individual or family to support charitable activities through grants. It is governed by its own board of trustees, usually comprising family members and close associates, offering greater control over how funds are distributed. On the other hand, a charitable trust is a fiduciary relationship in which a trustee holds and manages assets for the benefit of a charitable cause. Charitable trusts often provide more immediate tax benefits but offer less control to the donor regarding the specifics of how funds are utilized.

Next, let's look at the steps required to establish a family foundation. The process begins with deciding the type of foundation, either private or public. Private foundations are usually funded by a single source, such as a family, while public foundations receive funding from multiple sources, including the general public. Both types have distinct regulatory requirements; therefore, it's essential to choose the one that aligns best with your philanthropic goals.

Once you've determined the type of foundation, you'll need to handle the legal aspects of establishment, which include drafting articles of incorporation and bylaws. These documents outline the foundation's purpose, governance structure, and operational guidelines. It's wise to consult with a legal advisor specializing in nonprofit law during this phase to ensure compliance with federal and state laws. Additionally, filing for tax-exempt status with the IRS is crucial. This involves completing Form 1023 for private foundations, which requires detailed information about the foundation's proposed operations, financial data, and governance structure.

Governance is another critical aspect to consider when establishing a family foundation. The board of trustees plays a pivotal role in overseeing the foundation's activities and ensuring that it remains focused on its mission. Selecting trustees who are passionate about the foundation's goals and possess a diverse range of skills is imperative for long-term success. Moreover, establishing clear policies and procedures for grantmaking, conflict of interest, and financial oversight ensures transparency and accountability within the organization.

It's also important to account for potential costs involved in setting up and maintaining a family foundation. Initial setup fees include legal and accounting services, filing fees for incorporating and obtaining tax-exempt status, and potentially, costs for initial fundraising efforts. Ongoing operational expenses, such as administrative costs, staff salaries (if applicable), and audit fees, should also be factored into your budget.

Once the structural and legal foundations are in place, defining the goals and mission of your family foundation becomes paramount. The mission statement serves as a guiding star, helping to focus the foundation's efforts and communicate its objectives to potential donors and partners. When crafting a mission statement, consider what social issues or causes resonate most deeply with your family. An effective mission statement should be clear, concise, and inspirational, encapsulating the essence of your foundation's purpose and the impact it aims to achieve. For example, if your family is passionate about education, your mission might be to "empower underprivileged youth through access to quality educational resources and opportunities."

In addition to a strong mission statement, setting specific, measurable goals will help track the foundation's progress and maintain alignment with its overarching objectives. These goals could range from funding a certain number of scholarships annually to supporting research projects that address pressing societal challenges. By clearly articulating these goals, you not only enhance the foundation's strategic focus but also demonstrate commitment to potential supporters and beneficiaries.

Involving family members in the activities of the foundation can greatly enhance its effectiveness and sustainability. Engaging family members fosters a sense of shared responsibility and collective purpose, ensuring that the foundation's vision extends beyond the founding generation. Begin by encouraging family participation in decision-making processes, such as selecting grant recipients or approving major initiatives. This inclusion not only leverages diverse perspectives and expertise but also strengthens family bonds through a shared commitment to philanthropy.

Moreover, involving younger family members early on can cultivate a lifelong culture of giving and social responsibility. Consider creating structured programs, like family retreats or workshops, where younger members can learn about the foundation's work, understand the importance of charitable giving, and develop essential skills in leadership and governance. Mentorship opportunities, where seasoned trustees guide newer or younger family members, can also be valuable in fostering continuity and preserving the foundation's values across generations.

Another effective strategy for family engagement is to establish committees that focus on different aspects of the foundation's operations, such as community outreach, grant evaluation, or event planning. Assigning roles based on individual interests and strengths not only increases involvement but also enhances the overall functionality of the foundation.

Finally, maintain open lines of communication within the family to discuss the foundation's progress, challenges, and future direction. Regular meetings, whether formal board sessions or informal gatherings, provide a platform for dialogue, feedback, and collaborative decision-making.

Incorporating Philanthropy into Legacy Planning

One of the most effective ways to ensure your legacy endures and makes a lasting impact is by integrating charitable giving into your estate planning. This can create a synergy between your financial goals and your philanthropic intentions, enabling you to leave both a financial and moral inheritance. For many, charitable giving is not just a financial choice but an expression of values and life principles.

Aligning Financial Goals with Charitable Intentions

The first step in seamless philanthropic integration is aligning your financial goals with your charitable intentions. Before diving into specific strategies, consider what causes resonate most with you. Whether it's education, healthcare, environmental conservation, or social justice, your passions should guide your giving. Once you've identified these causes, examine how charitable contributions can complement your broader financial objectives.

For instance, donating appreciated assets such as stocks can reduce your capital gains tax while providing significant funds to your chosen charity. Additionally, charitable contributions can offer income tax deductions, which could help offset other taxable income. Thus, charitable giving not only fulfills altruistic desires but can also serve to streamline your financial portfolio effectively.

It's essential to conduct a thorough financial review to understand your asset base and liquidity needs, ensuring that your charitable plans are sustainable without compromising your financial security. By setting clear financial targets and evaluating them regularly, you can make informed decisions that benefit both your heirs and your charitable beneficiaries.

Structuring Gifts for Maximum Impact

Once you've aligned your charitable goals with your financial objectives, the next step is structuring your gifts in a way that maximizes their impact. Several strategies can be employed to ensure that your charitable donations are both meaningful and effective.

One approach is to establish a donor-advised fund (DAF), which allows you to make a charitable contribution, receive an immediate tax deduction, and then recommend grants from the fund over time. Another strategy is creating charitable remainder trusts (CRTs) or charitable lead trusts (CLTs). These vehicles provide a stream of income either to you or the charity for a specified period, after which the remaining assets are transferred to the designated beneficiaries.

Additionally, lifetime giving can be structured to take advantage of annual gift tax exclusions and other benefits, making it possible to support your chosen causes while enjoying potential tax savings. You might also consider making direct gifts to charities during your lifetime, which allows you to see the impact of your generosity firsthand and adjust your giving strategy as needed.

Engaging Legal and Financial Advisors

Navigating the complexities of charitable giving within the framework of estate planning often requires professional guidance. Engaging legal and financial advisors who specialize in this area is crucial. These professionals can offer valuable insight into the legalities and tax implications of various charitable giving options.

A seasoned estate planning attorney can help draft necessary documents, ensuring that your charitable intentions are clearly articulated and legally binding. A financial advisor, on the other hand, can provide recommendations on investment strategies that align with your philanthropic goals while maintaining overall financial health.

Regular consultations with your advisors can help keep your estate plan current, especially in light of changes in tax laws and personal circumstances such as marriage, divorce, or significant shifts in your financial standing. Professionals can also offer advice on the best practices for documenting your charitable intentions to avoid any potential disputes among heirs or beneficiaries.

Communicating Your Vision

An often-overlooked aspect of integrating philanthropy into estate planning is communicating your vision to your heirs and loved ones. Transparent communication ensures that your charitable goals are honored and can even inspire future generations to continue your legacy of giving.

Begin by having open discussions with your family about the causes that matter most to you and why you've chosen to support them. Share your specific plans and the mechanisms you've set up to achieve your philanthropic objectives. This might include explaining the purpose and function of any trusts, donor-advised funds, or direct gifts you've established.

Presenting a written statement of your charitable vision can be a powerful tool. This document should outline not only the logistics of your philanthropic efforts but also the values and motivations behind your choices. Including this in your estate planning documentation can serve as a guiding principle for your heirs, providing clarity and direction for honoring your intentions.

In some cases, involving family members directly in the decision-making process can foster a shared commitment to the causes you care about. Encouraging family members to participate in charitable activities or serve on the boards of foundations can deepen their understanding of your philanthropic legacy and strengthen familial bonds around shared values.

Integrating charitable giving into your estate planning is a multifaceted endeavor that requires careful consideration and strategic execution. By aligning your financial goals with your charitable intentions, structuring your gifts for maximum impact, engaging professional advisors, and clearly communicating your vision to your heirs, you can create a lasting legacy that reflects your values and makes a meaningful difference in the world.

Whether you're beginning to contemplate your estate planning options or looking to update an existing plan, embracing these strategies can help ensure that your philanthropic efforts are seamlessly integrated into your overall legacy planning. The result is a balanced approach that protects your financial interests, supports the causes you cherish, and provides clear guidance for your heirs to follow.

In this chapter, we have explored various planned giving options that can help integrate philanthropy into estate planning. By understanding the benefits and intricacies of bequests, retirement accounts, donor-advised funds, and charitable remainder trusts, you can align your financial goals with meaningful contributions to causes you care about. Each option offers unique advantages and flexibility, enabling you to make a lasting impact while also providing potential tax benefits and efficient asset distribution.

As we conclude, it is clear that incorporating charitable giving into your estate plan requires careful consideration and strategic planning. Engaging with legal and financial advisors ensures that your philanthropic intentions are effectively executed, while ongoing communication with family members helps maintain a shared vision of generosity across generations. By thoughtfully combining these elements, you can create a legacy that not only reflects your values but also supports future generations in a meaningful way.

CHAPTER 13

Navigating Legislative Changes

Navigating legislative changes is a fundamental aspect of maintaining a legally sound and effective estate plan. The fluid nature of laws governing estate planning makes it imperative to understand how they can impact your carefully laid plans. Without adaptation, these changes can compromise the protections and benefits you have established for your beneficiaries. Those who wish to secure their financial future must stay informed and proactive in updating their estate plans to reflect new legal requirements.

In this chapter, we will explore the strategies necessary to adapt your estate plan to evolving legislative landscapes. First, we will discuss how to reliably monitor and interpret new laws, ensuring you stay ahead of potential changes that could affect your assets. Additionally, we will delve into specific examples of recent legislative shifts and their direct impacts on estate planning, offering clear insights into the necessity for timely updates. By focusing on expert advice and practical tools, readers will gain valuable knowledge on how to effectively manage their estate plans amidst continuous regulatory changes.

Monitoring Legislative Changes

In the dynamic landscape of estate planning, staying abreast of legislative changes is crucial for safeguarding your financial future. One effective strategy involves identifying and accessing trustworthy resources that provide legislative updates. Reliable sources include government websites, legal publications, and professional organizations. These entities often offer timely and accurate information about new laws and regulations. Subscribing to their newsletters or attending webinars can ensure that you receive updates directly from authoritative bodies. Additionally, working with a qualified estate planning attorney can help you stay informed, as they are typically well-versed in current legislative developments.

Understanding the importance of staying up-to-date with local, state, and federal changes is essential for ensuring compliance with evolving laws. Each jurisdiction may have unique regulations affecting various aspects of estate planning, such as inheritance taxes, trust management, and asset distribution. It is vital to be aware of any modifications that could impact your plans. For instance, changes in state tax laws might influence how your assets are taxed after your passing. Similarly, new federal regulations could affect the benefits available to special needs beneficiaries. By staying informed, you can make necessary adjustments to your estate plan, ensuring it remains effective and legally sound.

Monitoring legislative changes effectively can prevent unpleasant surprises that might otherwise disrupt your estate plan. Imagine discovering too late that a change in the law has nullified a key component of your estate plan, leaving your heirs unprotected or facing significant tax liabilities. Proactive monitoring allows you to anticipate and address potential issues before they become problematic. For example, if a new law restricts certain types of trusts, knowing this in advance enables you to explore alternative strategies with your legal advisor. This approach not only safeguards your assets but also provides peace of mind, knowing that your estate plan is always up-to-date and compliant with the latest regulations.

Leveraging technology can significantly simplify the process of keeping track of legal changes. There are numerous tools and applications designed to help individuals monitor legislative developments relevant to estate planning. Legal news apps, for example, can send real-time notifications about changes in estate planning laws. Some financial planning software solutions also include features that highlight pertinent legislative updates. Moreover, social media platforms like LinkedIn and Twitter can be valuable resources for following legal experts and professional organizations. These platforms often share insights and analyses about recent legislative changes, making it easier for you to stay informed without extensive research.

Utilizing these technological tools not only streamlines the process of tracking legislative updates but also ensures that you remain proactive in managing your estate plan. Regularly reviewing alerts and notifications can help you quickly identify any changes that may require attention. Additionally, many of these tools offer customizable settings, allowing you to focus on specific areas of interest, such as tax laws or trust regulations. This targeted approach ensures that you receive relevant information, enabling you to act swiftly and make informed decisions about your estate plan.

For families with minor children or special needs beneficiaries, staying informed about legislative changes is particularly important. Laws governing guardianships, conservatorships, and special needs trusts can have significant implications for these groups. By actively tracking changes in these areas, you can ensure that your estate plan continues to provide the necessary protections and support for your dependents. For example, if a new law introduces additional benefits for special needs trusts, incorporating these changes into your estate plan can enhance the financial security of your loved ones.

Similarly, individuals experiencing life changes, such as marriage, divorce, or the acquisition of significant assets, must remain vigilant about legislative updates. Changes in family structure or financial status can necessitate revisions to your estate plan to reflect your current circumstances accurately. For instance, new legislation affecting spousal rights or property division in divorce cases can impact how your assets are distributed. Keeping track of these developments ensures that your estate plan remains aligned with your intentions and legal requirements.

Impact on Existing Plans

Legislative changes can have profound impacts on estate plans, making it crucial to stay informed and adapt accordingly. One of the most effective ways to illustrate this is through examples of recent legislative changes that have directly affected estate planning.

Consider the Tax Cuts and Jobs Act of 2017, which significantly altered the federal estate tax exemption, doubling it from $5.49 million to over $11 million per individual. This change had substantial implications for many families, especially those who previously fell within the taxable estate range but no longer did under the new law. Estate plans that included strategies to minimize estate taxes—such as gifting or establishing certain trusts—needed reevaluation. Families could now potentially retain more assets without incurring hefty tax burdens, demonstrating a clear advantage provided by the legislative shift.

However, not all changes offer benefits. For instance, the implementation of the Setting Every Community Up for Retirement Enhancement (SECURE) Act in 2020 eliminated the "stretch" IRA provision, which allowed non-spouse beneficiaries to extend distributions over their lifetime. This alteration necessitated a revamp of estate plans that relied on the stretch IRA strategy for tax-efficient wealth transfer and required beneficiaries to withdraw inherited IRAs within ten years, accelerating tax liabilities.

Understanding specific changes like these helps demystify the legislative process, making it more accessible to those planning their estates. By examining real-world examples, readers can better comprehend how laws influence their planning decisions, whether by presenting new opportunities or imposing unexpected constraints.

Changes in tax laws are often at the forefront of legislative impacts on estate planning. Revisions in income tax rates, capital gains taxes, and estate tax exemptions can all necessitate reassessments of existing plans. For example, if a state enacts or repeals an estate or inheritance tax, residents must adjust their strategies accordingly. A case in point is Minnesota, where recent adjustments to estate tax exemptions have caused residents to reconsider their estate tax exposure and explore different planning techniques, such as gifting during their lifetime or setting up resident trusts in states with more favorable tax laws.

Educating oneself on how often to check for updates can keep plans current. It's not just about reacting to changes after they happen but being proactive in anticipating how potential legislative shifts might affect one's estate plan. Staying informed about proposed bills or amendments up for vote allows individuals to consult with their legal advisors and make proactive adjustments before laws are set in stone. Regularly reviewing estate plans in light of legislative sessions ensures that they remain compliant and optimized.

Consider the continuously changing landscape of healthcare legislation, which can impact special needs trusts designed to benefit individuals with disabilities. Any modifications to Medicaid or other public benefits could disrupt the carefully laid plans of families aiming to provide long-term financial security for their dependents. For instance, changes in the eligibility requirements for Medicaid could alter the effectiveness of an established trust, requiring revisions to ensure continued support without jeopardizing benefits.

Highlighting such legislative changes underscores the importance of timely adaptation. Delayed adjustments can lead to noncompliance and disrupt beneficiaries' financial security. A particularly illustrative case involved a family that failed to update their estate plan after significant tax law changes. Upon the death of the primary breadwinner, the family faced unexpected tax liabilities that could have been avoided with a reassessment of their plan. The resulting financial strain underscored the necessity of regular review and adjustment in response to legislative evolution.

To provide further context, consider the impact of changes in charitable giving regulations. Recent legislative updates have introduced additional incentives for charitable contributions, increasing the deduction limits for cash donations to qualified organizations. For philanthropically inclined individuals, these changes present a prime opportunity to revise their estate plans, maximizing the benefits for both their beneficiaries and favored charities. However, failing to incorporate these updates means missing out on advantageous deductions, ultimately reducing the estate's efficiency.

Understanding the nuances of legislative changes also helps readers grasp why ongoing education is vital. Legislative jargon and complex statutes can overwhelm even the most astute planners. Breaking down these changes into manageable insights helps demystify the process. For example, explaining the differences between revocable and irrevocable trusts in light of updated trust regulations can aid individuals in choosing the best structure for their needs and ensuring their assets are protected according to the latest laws.

In essence, continuous learning about developments in estate planning laws provides readers with the knowledge needed to maintain compliant and effective plans. Highlighting the tangible effects of legislative changes reinforces the necessity of vigilance and adaptability. Whether through increased tax exemptions, revised retirement account rules, or new incentives for charitable giving, legislative shifts present both challenges and opportunities that require careful navigation.

Proactive Adjustments

Establishing a regular review schedule for your estate plans is crucial to ensuring they remain effective and legally sound amidst constantly evolving legislative changes. It can be tempting to set up an estate plan and forget about it, assuming that once it's done, it's done for good. However, laws and personal circumstances change over time, and failing to update your plans accordingly could leave your assets unprotected or cause unintended consequences for your beneficiaries.

Creating a review schedule involves setting aside specific times to revisit and assess your estate plan. This doesn't need to be a daunting task; rather, think of it as a proactive approach to safeguarding your future wishes. Setting a bi-annual or annual date to review your estate plan can help make this part of your routine. Using specific dates like a birthday or the beginning of a new year can serve as easy reminders to check if any updates are needed.

Having a scheduled review process embedded into your calendar can transform what might seem like a cumbersome task into a manageable and standard practice. This habit ensures that you are always aware of both major and minor changes in legislation that could directly impact your estate plan. By making these reviews a routine, you create an opportunity to regularly consult with your attorney, financial advisor, or both, ensuring all legal documents reflect current laws and your most recent life circumstances.

Routine assessments also offer significant benefits beyond mere compliance with the law. They can lead to the discovery of more efficient ways to manage and distribute your assets. When routinely evaluating your estate plan, you might identify gaps or areas that need adjustment due to new investments, changes in family dynamics, or shifts in your personal goals. Such ongoing evaluations encourage a proactive mindset, which can be empowering. Rather than feeling overwhelmed by the prospect of estate planning, you take control, knowing that each assessment keeps your plans relevant and robust.

To simplify this process further, consider using tools like calendars or checklists. These tools can be invaluable in guiding you through each review session. A well-thought-out checklist can provide step-by-step guidance on what documents to review, questions to ask, and aspects to consider during the evaluation. For example, your checklist could include verifying beneficiary designations, reviewing wills and trusts, updating power of attorney and healthcare directives, and confirming asset titles align with your estate plan.

A physical or digital calendar acts as a straightforward but powerful reminder system. Scheduling review sessions in advance ensures that you never overlook this critical task. Many people find that integrating these sessions into existing routines helps them stick to their schedule more faithfully. For instance, linking the review to tax season can be particularly effective, as you're already gathering financial information and thinking about your fiscal situation.

By creating a structured yet flexible approach, you demystify the process and reduce the risk of oversight. This structure allows you to address smaller, incremental changes over time, rather than facing a massive overhaul all at once. It also offers peace of mind, knowing that your estate plan evolves alongside your needs and the legal landscape.

It's worth noting that even small changes in the law can have a profound impact on your estate plan. Therefore, staying informed about these changes through periodic reviews is not just recommended; it's essential. For instance, changes in federal estate tax laws, inheritance laws, and state-specific regulations can alter how your assets are distributed and taxed. Without regular updates, you may inadvertently leave your estate vulnerable to greater taxation or legal challenges, which can diminish the inheritance intended for your loved ones.

One of the most compelling arguments for establishing a review schedule is the potential to prevent costly disputes among beneficiaries. Clear, updated, and legally compliant estate plans minimize ambiguities, reducing the chances of misunderstandings or conflicts amongst family members. Regular updates ensure that your intentions are explicitly documented, thereby protecting your beneficiaries from potential legal battles.

Additionally, the legislative landscape is not static. Governments frequently amend tax laws, probate codes, and other regulations that influence estate planning. What was adequate protection five years ago might now be insufficient under current laws. By fostering a routine schedule of reviews, you maintain a dynamic estate plan that adapts to legislative changes seamlessly.

For those who prefer a high-tech solution, numerous digital tools and apps can help manage your schedule and document updates efficiently. Some platforms offer alerts and notifications for upcoming reviews, centralized storage for your estate documents, and even integrate with financial management software to provide a holistic view of your assets. The convenience of digital solutions can be particularly beneficial in maintaining consistent review schedules.

Incorporating these practices doesn't only benefit the individuals directly involved; it also sets a positive example for future generations. It underscores the importance of being diligent and proactive about managing one's affairs, which can foster a culture of responsibility and foresight within families.

Engaging Legal Professionals

Collaborating with legal experts in estate planning is not just an option but a necessity for individuals aiming to ensure that their estate plans remain effective and compliant in the face of evolving laws. As legislative changes can significantly impact the validity and integrity of estate plans, working with knowledgeable professionals provides the best defense against unforeseen legal challenges. This subpoint explores the critical role of selecting qualified estate planning attorneys, the importance of engaging these professionals, identifying red flags to avoid poor experiences, and leveraging community networks and referrals for finding the right legal advisers.

Choosing the right professionals is the cornerstone of successful estate planning. When looking for a qualified estate planning attorney, several criteria should be considered. Firstly, verify their specialization in estate law; this ensures that they possess the specific expertise required. Experience is equally important; an attorney with a track record of handling estate planning issues will likely navigate complex legal landscapes more effectively. Licensing and certifications also matter—ensure that the attorney is recognized by reputable professional bodies. It's prudent to check their educational background and ongoing training in estate law. Client testimonials and reviews can provide insights into the attorney's competence and reliability.

Once the right professionals are identified, the value of engaging knowledgeable legal people becomes apparent. A seasoned estate planning attorney ensures that your estate plan complies with current laws and regulations, providing peace of mind. They can identify potential legal pitfalls and offer solutions tailored to your unique circumstances, safeguarding your assets for future generations. With their up-to-date knowledge of legislative changes, these experts can proactively adjust your estate plan to align with new laws, preventing costly legal battles and complications.

However, not all legal advisers possess the dedication and expertise needed for meticulous estate planning. Recognizing and avoiding red flags is essential to prevent poor experiences. Be wary of advisors who lack transparency in their fees or those who promise guaranteed outcomes—estate law involves numerous variables, and ethical professionals understand the complexity. A disorganized office or poor communication skills can also indicate inefficiency and unreliability. Additionally, any reluctance to provide clear explanations about the process or their previous work should be a warning sign. Trustworthy attorneys prioritize client education and clarity, ensuring you understand every aspect of your estate plan.

To streamline the search for a qualified estate planning attorney, utilizing community networks and seeking referrals can be incredibly beneficial. Word-of-mouth recommendations from friends, family, or colleagues who have had positive experiences with estate planning attorneys can save time and provide assurance of quality service. Professional associations and local bar associations often have directories and referral services that list qualified attorneys specializing in estate planning. Engaging with online forums and social media groups dedicated to estate planning can also yield valuable suggestions and reviews.

Assessing Your Current Plan

Identifying areas of existing estate plans that may require changes due to new regulations is crucial in ensuring they remain effective and legally sound. This process begins with conducting regular assessments, which can uncover vulnerabilities before they become liabilities. By evaluating your current estate plan periodically, you can identify aspects that are likely affected by recent legislative changes.

Regular assessments not only provide a snapshot of the current standing of your estate plan but also highlight potential risks that could compromise its effectiveness. These assessments should be conducted at least annually or whenever significant life events occur, such as marriage, divorce, birth of a child, or acquiring substantial assets. Through this practice, you stay ahead of changes and avoid unexpected complications that could arise from outdated provisions.

To empower readers, it's beneficial to demonstrate a systematic approach to reviewing their estate plans. Begin by gathering all relevant documents related to wills, trusts, power of attorney, and beneficiary designations. Creating a checklist can streamline this process, ensuring no essential component is overlooked. This organized method not only reduces confusion but also provides a clear path for making necessary updates.

In addition to organization, knowing where to focus your review efforts is vital. Key areas such as tax implications and asset distribution often undergo legislative alterations. For instance, changes in tax laws can significantly impact the overall value that beneficiaries receive from an estate. Staying informed about these key areas helps prioritize reviews and ensures compliance with new regulations. By concentrating on high-impact areas like taxes and asset distribution, you can address the most critical components of your estate plan first.

It's also useful to understand the real consequences of noncompliance with new laws. Not adjusting your estate plan to reflect legislative changes can lead to unintended tax burdens, legal disputes among heirs, or even invalidation of certain provisions. Sharing examples of real-world cases where failure to adapt resulted in significant losses can serve as a powerful motivator. For instance, consider an individual who didn't update their will after major tax law changes, resulting in hefty estate taxes that diminished the intended inheritance for heirs.

Another critical element is recognizing the specific needs of different types of beneficiaries and how new regulations might affect them. Families with minor children or special needs beneficiaries, for example, must be particularly vigilant. These groups often require tailored strategies for long-term financial security and asset management, possibly involving special needs trusts or guardianship arrangements that are compliant with current laws. Regularly reassessing these factors ensures that all beneficiaries are adequately protected under the latest legal framework.

Moreover, providing guidelines on how to execute these assessments effectively can further aid readers. Here are some steps to consider:

1. **Schedule Regular Reviews:** Mark your calendar for annual or bi-annual reviews of your estate plan. Consistency ensures you stay on top of any necessary adjustments.

1. **Create a Comprehensive Checklist:** List all essential documents and areas to review, including wills, trusts, power of attorney, and beneficiary designations. Tailor the checklist to include specific items pertinent to changes in laws affecting taxes and asset distribution.

1. **Consult Professionals:** Engage with estate planning attorneys or financial advisors who are well-versed in current laws. Their expertise can offer valuable insights and prevent costly mistakes.

1. **Document Changes:** Keep a record of all modifications made during each review. This preserves a history of your estate plan's evolution and offers clarity for future assessments.

1. **Communicate With Family:** Ensure close family members or designated executors are aware of the updates and the reasons behind them. Transparent communication can prevent disputes and ensure everyone understands the intent of your plan.

By following these guidelines, readers can confidently navigate the complexities of legislative changes and maintain effective estate plans. The act of regularly updating an estate plan not only aligns with legal requirements but also reflects the responsible management of one's legacy. Ensuring that your wishes are honored and your beneficiaries are cared for requires ongoing attention and commitment to adapting to new regulations.

Understanding the importance of regular assessments, demonstrating a systematic approach, focusing on critical areas, and recognizing the consequences of noncompliance equips individuals with the tools needed to manage their estate plans proactively. Avoiding complacency and embracing a proactive mindset can make a significant difference in preserving wealth and safeguarding the future of loved ones. The act of routinely evaluating and adjusting estate plans is an essential strategy in the broader context of comprehensive financial management.

Adapting your estate plan to comply with evolving laws is essential for ensuring its effectiveness and legality. Throughout this chapter, the importance of staying informed about legislative changes has been emphasized. By leveraging reliable resources such as government websites, legal publications, and professional organizations, you can receive timely updates on new laws and regulations. Working closely with a qualified estate planning attorney further ensures that your estate plan remains current and compliant.

Implementing regular reviews of your estate plan is crucial in adapting to legislative shifts. Scheduled assessments allow you to address potential issues proactively, preventing unforeseen complications that could impact your beneficiaries. Utilizing technological tools and applications can simplify the process of monitoring legal changes. This proactive approach not only protects your assets but also provides peace of mind, knowing that your estate plan evolves alongside changing laws and personal circumstances.

CHAPTER 14

Cost Optimization in Estate Planning

Cost optimization in estate planning involves implementing strategies to minimize expenses while ensuring robust protection for one's assets. It's essential to understand that effective estate planning doesn't have to be prohibitively expensive. By selecting cost-effective tools and resources, individuals can create comprehensive plans that safeguard their assets without depleting their financial reserves.

In this chapter, various strategies for minimizing costs in estate planning are discussed. Readers will learn about the benefits of using DIY estate planning software, which provides templates for personalizing wills and trusts. The chapter also explores the advantages of online legal services as affordable alternatives to traditional consultations. Additionally, community legal clinics and public records are highlighted as valuable resources for those seeking economical estate planning assistance. Each method is evaluated for its ability to reduce costs while offering necessary legal protections.

Selecting Cost-Effective Planning Tools

Cost optimization in estate planning is crucial for those looking to safeguard their assets without incurring substantial expenses. Affordable options for estate planning are available, and exploring these can help ensure that financial resources are spent wisely while still achieving comprehensive protection for one's estate.

DIY estate planning software has become an increasingly popular option for those seeking cost-effective solutions. These tools provide templates for wills and trusts that can be tailored to individual needs. By using such software, individuals can save significant amounts in legal fees that would otherwise be spent on attorney consultations. The step-by-step guides included with the software help demystify the process, making it accessible even to those with little legal knowledge. This approach allows users to maintain a sense of control over their estate planning while ensuring that all necessary components are covered. For example, if you wish to include specific clauses concerning guardianship for minor children or directives for healthcare decisions, these software programs typically offer easy-to-use customization options.

Online legal services also present a viable alternative to traditional in-office consultations. These services offer customizable estate planning packages that often include virtual consultations with legal professionals. By eliminating the need for physical travel, online legal services reduce both time and transportation costs, making the process more convenient and affordable. These virtual platforms usually provide access to a range of documents, such as durable powers of attorney and advance health care directives, which can be tailored to fit specific needs. Additionally, clients can benefit from the expertise of licensed attorneys who are available to answer questions and provide guidance throughout the planning process.

Another resource to consider is community legal clinics, which often offer estate planning services at either no cost or at significantly reduced rates. Many community legal clinics are staffed by volunteer attorneys who provide pro bono services or work within a sliding fee scale based on the client's income. These clinics can assist with essential document preparation and provide valuable legal advice, ensuring that even those with limited financial resources have access to quality estate planning assistance. For families with special needs beneficiaries, this is particularly advantageous, as these clinics can help navigate the complexities of setting up special needs trusts and other relevant arrangements. Community legal clinics may also conduct workshops and free consultations on estate planning, helping individuals understand their options and take the first steps towards securing their estate.

Utilizing public records through local government offices is another effective strategy for minimizing costs associated with estate planning. Many local government offices provide access to educational resources and sample documents that can guide individuals through the planning process. Public libraries frequently house legal guides and estate planning forms that can be borrowed or accessed digitally. By leveraging these public resources, individuals can gain the knowledge needed to handle parts of the estate planning process independently. Furthermore, some regions offer public access to probate court records, which can serve as examples of how estates are managed and distributed. Observing the outcomes of similar cases can help individuals make informed decisions regarding their own estate plans.

Avoiding Probate Costs

When planning for estate management, minimizing probate expenses is crucial. Probate, the legal process of validating a will, can be costly and time-consuming. By employing strategic techniques, one can significantly reduce these expenses, ensuring that more assets are preserved for beneficiaries.

One effective technique is establishing living trusts. A living trust allows you to transfer ownership of your assets into the trust while you are still alive. This strategy helps avoid the probate process entirely. Because the assets are already placed in the trust, they pass directly to the beneficiaries upon your passing, without the need for court intervention. This not only speeds up the transfer but also keeps it private, as probate records are public. The creation and maintenance of a living trust may involve some initial costs, such as drafting fees and funding expenses, but these are often offset by the savings in probate costs and the peace of mind knowing that the assets will be distributed as intended.

Another way to bypass probate is through joint ownership of assets. When assets like real estate or bank accounts are jointly owned, they automatically pass to the surviving owner when one owner passes away. This form of ownership is particularly beneficial for married couples but can also be utilized by individuals in other relationships. For instance, adding a child as a joint owner to a property deed ensures that the property transfers seamlessly without entering the probate process. It's essential to understand the implications and limitations of joint ownership, especially concerning potential disputes among heirs and possible exposure to creditors of the joint owner.

Assigning beneficiaries to specific financial accounts, such as life insurance policies, retirement plans, or payable-on-death (POD) bank accounts, is another effective strategy. These beneficiary designations override any instructions in a will, allowing the funds to be transferred directly to the named individuals without passing through probate. This method ensures that the intended recipients receive the assets quickly and without additional legal hurdles. Regular updates to beneficiary designations are critical, especially after major life events like marriage, divorce, or the birth of a child, to ensure that the right individuals are named and there are no conflicts with other estate planning documents.

Gifting assets during one's lifetime is another viable option for reducing probate costs. By transferring ownership of certain assets before passing away, you can effectively decrease the size of your estate, thereby lowering the potential probate expenses. Gifting can also offer tax advantages if done correctly, as smaller estates might qualify for exclusions from estate taxes. However, gifting must be approached thoughtfully, considering the annual gift tax exclusion limits and the potential impact on both the giver and receiver's finances. For instance, gifting a valuable asset, such as a piece of property, could result in significant capital gains taxes for the recipient upon its eventual sale.

Each of these strategies offers distinct advantages and challenges. For example, while establishing a living trust provides comprehensive estate planning benefits, it requires careful drafting and proper funding to be effective. Joint ownership simplifies asset transfer but could complicate personal relationships if not planned appropriately. Beneficiary designations provide quick and direct asset transfer, requiring periodic reviews and updates to remain effective. Gifting reduces the taxable estate, needing careful consideration of gift tax implications and the overall financial impact.

These methods should be tailored to each individual's circumstances, balancing the need to minimize probate expenses with maintaining control over assets and ensuring fair distribution among heirs. Consulting with an estate planning professional is highly recommended to navigate these options effectively, as they can provide personalized advice based on current laws and individual goals. Through informed decisions and strategic planning, one can protect their estate economically, ensuring a smooth transition of assets to future generations.

Using DIY Templates Wisely

In the ever-evolving landscape of estate planning, leveraging DIY templates can offer an economical and practical alternative to hiring legal professionals for every step of the process. This approach, however, requires careful consideration to ensure that it achieves the desired outcome without leading to unintended complications later on. Here, we will explore key aspects of effectively using DIY templates, focusing on quality, customization, regular updates, and professional oversight.

First and foremost, the importance of selecting high-quality templates that comply with state laws cannot be overstated. Estate planning documents, such as wills and trusts, are governed by specific regulations that vary from state to state. Using a template that does not adhere to these regulations can render your documents invalid, potentially leading to disputes among heirs or beneficiaries. Therefore, when choosing a DIY template, it's crucial to ensure that it is up-to-date and tailored to the legal requirements of your state. Reputable sources often provide detailed descriptions of how their templates meet state-specific mandates, which can serve as a good starting point in your selection process. Additionally, user reviews and ratings can offer insights into the reliability and robustness of the template.

Once you have selected a high-quality template, personalizing it to accurately reflect your specific needs and unique situations is the next critical step. Estate plans are deeply personal and must account for various individual circumstances. For instance, blended families may need particular arrangements to ensure all heirs are treated equitably. Similarly, if you have dependents with special needs, your estate plan should include provisions for their long-term care and financial security. Customization might involve specifying guardianship for minor children, detailing the distribution of assets, or setting up special needs trusts. The ability to tailor these templates ensures that your estate plan aligns with your wishes and provides clear directives to your executors and beneficiaries.

Regularly revisiting and updating your templates to accommodate significant life events is equally important. Life is unpredictable, and changes such as marriage, divorce, the birth of a child, or shifts in asset values necessitate updating your estate plan to reflect new realities. An outdated estate plan can lead to confusion and potential legal battles among heirs. For example, failing to update a will after a divorce might unintentionally leave assets to an ex-spouse. Establishing a routine check-up once a year or following any major life event can help keep your estate plan current. This practice ensures that your intentions are clearly documented and that your assets are distributed in accordance with your latest wishes.

While DIY templates empower you to take control of your estate planning, having a legal professional review your documents before finalizing them provides an additional layer of protection. Even well-intentioned efforts can sometimes overlook subtle but significant legal nuances. A legal review can spot potential issues that might not be apparent to someone without a legal background. This kind of professional oversight helps correct errors and prevent future disputes, giving you and your beneficiaries peace of mind. It's a safeguard against common pitfalls, such as ambiguous language or improper execution of documents, which could otherwise invalidate your estate plan.

Trusted Financial Advisors

Consulting financial advisors can be integral to the estate planning process, providing a range of benefits that help ensure an individual's assets are protected and appropriately allocated. One of the key advantages is the selection of advisors with estate-specific expertise, as these professionals offer targeted advice aligned with specific financial goals.

Choosing the right advisor is crucial. Financial advisors focusing on estate planning possess in-depth knowledge about estate laws, tax implications, and asset management strategies. This specialized expertise allows them to craft tailored plans that maximize wealth preservation while ensuring compliance with legal requirements. For instance, they can recommend structures like trusts or charitable donations that might not be apparent to those without this specialized background. By doing so, they align the estate plan with broader financial objectives, such as providing for future generations or supporting philanthropic endeavors.

However, it's essential to understand different fee structures when selecting an advisor. Some advisors charge a flat fee for their services, which might be more predictable and easier to budget for. Others charge based on the value of the managed assets, potentially adding up if the estate's value increases over time. Understanding these fee structures helps clients choose advisors who offer the best value, ensuring that unexpected costs do not create financial strain. For instance, a flat fee arrangement could be more economical for individuals with significant assets, while percentage-based fees might benefit those with smaller estates. Assessing these options can lead to substantial savings and prevent future financial surprises.

Engaging a team approach by involving attorneys and accountants alongside financial advisors can significantly optimize estate planning decisions. Each professional brings unique expertise to the table—attorneys can provide valuable insights into legal frameworks and document creation, while accountants offer a deep understanding of tax implications and financial reporting. By collaborating, this multidisciplinary team ensures that all aspects of estate planning are comprehensively addressed.

For example, an attorney might draft a legally sound trust, while the accountant calculates potential tax benefits. Simultaneously, the financial advisor ensures that investments within the trust align with long-term financial goals. This collaborative effort reduces the risk of overlooking critical details and creates a more robust and efficient estate plan. Working together, these professionals can identify potential pitfalls, such as tax liabilities or legal challenges, before they become problematic.

Building ongoing relationships with advisors also proves invaluable. As personal circumstances change due to life events such as marriage, divorce, or the acquisition of new assets, having a trusted advisor facilitates timely updates to the estate plan. Advisors familiar with an individual's financial history and goals can provide relevant, personalized advice quickly, adapting the strategy as needed. This adaptability ensures the estate plan remains effective and aligned with current needs and objectives.

An advisor who knows the intricacies of one's financial situation can help navigate complex scenarios, such as blending families or managing special needs beneficiaries. Regular consultations also foster a proactive approach to estate planning, allowing for adjustments rather than reacting to changes. With this dynamic interaction, the estate plan continues to evolve, reflecting shifts in personal priorities and external factors like legislative changes.

In addition to these practical benefits, consulting financial advisors provides peace of mind. Knowing that a professional is guiding the estate planning process alleviates stress and uncertainty, allowing individuals to focus on other important aspects of their lives. The assurance that assets will be distributed according to one's wishes and that dependents will be provided for offers significant comfort.

Moreover, financial advisors often have access to advanced planning tools and software that streamline the planning process, making it more efficient and accurate. These resources can visualize how various strategies impact the overall estate, helping individuals make informed decisions. Utilizing such tools can uncover opportunities for tax savings or asset growth that might otherwise go unnoticed.

Utilizing Community Resources

Guiding readers to community resources offering cost-effective estate planning support can significantly reduce the expenses associated with creating and maintaining an estate plan. One of the most beneficial resources is local non-profits and volunteer organizations. These groups often host workshops and seminars on estate planning, which provide valuable information and tools. For example, many town councils or elder care organizations might organize events where experts discuss wills, trusts, powers of attorney, and more. Such sessions not only demystify the process but also offer attendees the chance to ask questions specific to their situations, thereby minimizing the need for costly one-on-one consultations.

Public libraries are another excellent resource for those seeking affordable help with estate planning. Many libraries offer access to legal forms and guides that individuals can use to complete estate planning documents independently. Libraries might also have book collections on estate planning, covering everything from the basics of drafting a will to more complex aspects like setting up a trust. By utilizing these materials, individuals can save on professional fees by preparing some documents themselves. Additionally, many libraries offer free internet access, allowing visitors to research further online resources or utilize digital forms and templates provided by reputable websites.

Universities and law schools often provide invaluable support through pro bono services offered by student legal clinics. These clinics are typically supervised by experienced attorneys, ensuring the quality of assistance remains high while giving law students practical experience. Individuals can receive help drafting estate documents, understand their rights, and navigate the often complex legal landscape at little to no cost. This symbiotic relationship benefits both the students, who gain essential hands-on learning, and the community members, who might otherwise be unable to afford such services.

Financial literacy programs in the community are another critical resource. These programs educate individuals on managing assets and planning estates, providing them with the knowledge needed to make informed decisions. For instance, community centers or non-profit financial counseling agencies often run classes or one-on-one sessions focusing on budgeting, saving, investing, and estate planning. Learning how to manage finances effectively helps ensure that any money spent on estate planning is well-utilized, maximizing the economic protection of one's assets.

In this chapter, we explored various strategies to keep estate planning costs manageable while still ensuring effective protection of your assets. We discussed the use of DIY templates and software, which allow for substantial savings by minimizing legal fees. The importance of choosing high-quality templates that adhere to state laws was emphasized, along with the need for personalization to fit individual circumstances. Furthermore, we highlighted the benefits of online legal services and community resources, such as workshops and public libraries, which offer valuable support at reduced or no cost.

We also covered methods to avoid probate expenses, including the establishment of living trusts and the strategic use of joint ownership and beneficiary designations. The advantages of gifting assets during one's lifetime were outlined as another means to reduce probate costs. Throughout these discussions, the emphasis remained on making informed decisions and seeking professional advice when necessary to ensure your estate plan is both economical and comprehensive. By employing these cost-effective strategies, you can secure your assets and provide for future generations without incurring unnecessary expenses.

CHAPTER 15

Ethical and Family Considerations

Balancing family dynamics and ethical obligations in estate distribution is a critical task that requires careful consideration. It involves navigating complex relationships, honoring personal wishes, and ensuring fair treatment of all beneficiaries. The process can be fraught with potential conflicts and misunderstandings if not handled with transparency and empathy. Effective communication and well-documented decisions are key to preventing disputes and maintaining harmony within the family. Taking into account each individual's unique circumstances and needs can further promote a sense of fairness and acceptance among heirs.

This chapter delves into several strategies for achieving this delicate balance. It begins by emphasizing the importance of open family discussions to foster understanding and alleviate concerns about estate plans. The role of clear documentation in reinforcing verbal agreements is also explored, highlighting how written records can provide concrete evidence of one's intentions. The chapter includes insights on involving legal professionals to ensure the comprehensiveness and legality of the estate plan. Additionally, it discusses the benefits of incorporating ethical guidelines, such as charitable giving and responsible asset management, to align with family values and traditions. Techniques for addressing past grievances and preventing future disputes are also covered to pave the way for a smoother execution of the estate plan. These combined efforts aim to create a fair, transparent, and harmonious approach to estate distribution.

Communicating Your Wishes

Open family discussions foster understanding and alleviate concerns by encouraging dialogue about estate plans. Proactively communicating your intentions regarding estate distribution can significantly reduce the emotional strain on loved ones. When family members are left in the dark, they may fill the gaps with assumptions, potentially leading to misunderstandings and conflicts. By discussing your plans openly, you create an atmosphere of transparency where questions can be raised, and concerns addressed.

Consider setting up a family meeting where everyone feels comfortable sharing their thoughts and feelings. Each individual's perspective can provide valuable insights that you might not have considered. This collaborative approach strengthens family bonds and assures each member that their voice is heard and valued in the process. Allowing family members to contribute to the discussion makes it easier for them to accept the final decisions, even if they don't entirely agree with them.

Documentation of intentions reinforces verbal discussions and serves as a reference point, ensuring clarity. While open conversations are crucial, they should be accompanied by clear documentation of your estate planning decisions. Written records provide concrete evidence of your wishes, which can be particularly important if disputes arise after your passing.

A well-documented estate plan should include a will, trusts, and any other pertinent legal documents that outline the distribution of your assets. These documents should be detailed and specific, leaving little room for ambiguity. Furthermore, explaining the reasoning behind your decisions in these documents can help prevent misunderstandings. For instance, if one child is receiving a larger share of your estate due to their financial needs or contributions to your care, clarifying this can mitigate feelings of favoritism or resentment among other heirs.

Engaging a mediator can facilitate sensitive discussions, introducing techniques to express grievances productively. Family dynamics can be complex, and discussions about estate planning can sometimes bring underlying tensions to the surface. A neutral third party, such as a mediator, can provide a safe space for all parties to express their feelings without fear of judgment or escalation.

Mediators are trained to handle emotionally charged situations and can guide the conversation in a constructive direction. They use strategies to ensure that everyone has an opportunity to speak and that grievances are expressed respectfully. For example, a mediator might employ techniques like active listening and empathy-building exercises to help family members understand each other's perspectives better. The goal is to reach a consensus that honors your wishes while maintaining harmony within the family.

Regular updates keep everyone informed about changes, helping align family members with your evolving intentions. Estate plans are not static; they should evolve over time to reflect changes in your circumstances and relationships. Life events such as marriage, divorce, the birth of a child, or the acquisition of new assets can all necessitate revisions to your plan.

Keeping your family informed about these updates ensures that there are no surprises down the line. Schedule regular check-ins with your loved ones to discuss any modifications to your estate plan. These updates not only keep everyone on the same page but also demonstrate your ongoing commitment to transparency and inclusivity. It reassures your family that their opinions and concerns continue to be important to you.

Preventing Family Disputes

Creating a fair process for estate distribution is the cornerstone of mitigating potential conflicts and ensuring that everyone's decisions are respected. When people feel they have been treated fairly, there's a higher chance of maintaining harmonious relationships among heirs. To start, it's crucial to communicate openly with family members about your intentions and reasons behind the estate plan. This transparency reduces misunderstandings and feelings of favoritism. Establishing clear guidelines for how assets will be distributed prevents future disputes and provides a sense of fairness among all involved parties.

To create a fair process, consider involving heirs during the planning stages. Asking for their input can make them feel valued and acknowledged, fostering an environment where everyone's perspectives are considered. This doesn't mean you have to follow every suggestion, but merely showing that you care about their opinions can go a long way in preventing resentment later on. Additionally, documenting each step of the process ensures there is a written record that can serve as a reference point, further validating the fairness of your actions.

Engagement of legal professionals plays an essential role in making sure that your estate plan is not only comprehensive but also legally binding. Consulting an estate attorney can help navigate the complexities of estate laws and ensure compliance with state regulations, which vary widely. A lawyer can assist in drafting wills, trusts, and other legal documents that clearly outline your distribution plans and minimize ambiguities. They can also provide advice on tax implications, helping maximize the estate's value while minimizing liabilities for your heirs.

Legal professionals bring an unbiased perspective to the table, helping you make decisions that are fair and justifiable. Their expertise ensures that your estate plan stands up to legal scrutiny, reducing the likelihood of contested wills and protracted court battles, which can strain familial relationships and drain financial resources. Moreover, they can guide you through contingency planning, ensuring that your wishes are carried out even if unforeseen circumstances arise.

Incorporating family values into your estate plan helps unify rather than divide, as it focuses on collective priorities and shared principles. Every family has its unique set of values and beliefs, and integrating these into your planning can foster a sense of unity and purpose. For instance, if philanthropy is a core family value, you might allocate a portion of the estate to charitable donations, demonstrating a commitment to causes that matter to everyone. This not only honors your values but also sets a precedent for future generations to continue the legacy of giving.

Highlighting shared experiences and traditions within the estate plan can also strengthen family bonds. By allocating heirlooms or meaningful possessions based on sentimental value rather than monetary worth, you emphasize the importance of family history and relationships. Discussing these allocations with family members beforehand can help ensure that everyone understands the significance behind each decision, promoting acceptance and reducing the potential for conflict.

Addressing past grievances before your passing is crucial for breaking patterns that often lead to disputes. Unresolved issues and lingering resentments can surface during the emotionally charged period following a loved one's death, exacerbating tensions and leading to conflicts over the estate. Proactively addressing these issues can pave the way for healing and reconciliation, creating a more peaceful environment for executing your estate plan.

One effective approach is to engage in honest and open conversations with family members to resolve any underlying conflicts. This might involve acknowledging past mistakes, offering apologies, and seeking forgiveness. While these discussions can be challenging, they are vital for mending relationships and ensuring a smoother transition when the time comes to distribute the estate. In some cases, it may be beneficial to seek the assistance of a mediator or family therapist to facilitate these conversations, providing a neutral space for everyone to express their feelings and work towards resolution.

By addressing grievances and fostering an atmosphere of understanding and empathy, you lay the groundwork for a more harmonious execution of your estate plan. Heirs who feel heard and valued are more likely to respect your decisions and support one another during the grieving process, preserving family unity and honoring your legacy.

Fair vs. Equal Distribution

Exploring the nuanced difference between fairness and equality in estate distribution is crucial for maintaining harmony and respecting individual circumstances within a family. When planning an estate, it's important to recognize that treating beneficiaries equally and treating them fairly are not always the same thing. Fairness often requires a deeper understanding of each individual's unique needs and circumstances.

A successful approach begins with understanding the individual needs of each beneficiary. This means thoroughly assessing their current financial situation, prospects, personal challenges, and any special requirements they may have. For instance, one child might have substantial medical expenses due to a chronic illness, while another might be financially independent but working in a lower-paying profession. By designating resources based on these unique circumstances, you can ensure that the distribution of the estate addresses the actual needs of each family member rather than simply dividing the assets equally. This tailored approach respects their individuality and promotes a more balanced and supportive environment.

Providing justification for these decisions is equally important. When beneficiaries understand the rationale behind the distributions, they are more likely to accept and respect your choices. Explaining your decisions can prevent feelings of resentment or unfairness. For example, if one child receives a larger share of the estate due to significant financial hardship, this should be communicated clearly to the other beneficiaries. Transparency helps mitigate misunderstandings and ensures that everyone is aware of the considerations taken into account. It might also be helpful to document your reasoning, providing a written explanation that beneficiaries can refer to, thus fostering acceptance and reducing potential conflicts.

Considering future needs is another critical aspect of fair estate distribution. The goal is to prioritize assets that accommodate foreseeable future requirements. For example, setting aside funds for a grandchild's education could be more beneficial than an immediate cash gift. Similarly, allocating part of the estate to support an adult child with ongoing care needs can align distributions with future challenges. By anticipating and planning for these needs, you help secure the long-term well-being of your beneficiaries. Assets like trusts can be particularly useful here, offering a structured way to manage and distribute wealth according to future necessities.

One effective method to convey your intentions and promote understanding among your beneficiaries is creating a letter of wishes. This personal document allows you to detail your thoughts, intentions, and the reasons behind your decisions. Unlike legal documents, a letter of wishes is more informal but can provide valuable insight and context. It adds a human touch to your estate plan, enabling your beneficiaries to see beyond the figures and legal jargon to understand your true intentions. In this letter, you can express your hopes for how the assets will be used and the values you hope to impart. This can be a powerful tool in bridging the gap between conception and perception, ensuring your wishes are honored and respected in the spirit you intended.

Including Ethical Guidelines

Ethical considerations in estate distribution are vital for maintaining family harmony, honoring family values and traditions, and ensuring the responsible management of inherited assets. The ethical principles guiding these decisions should be grounded in a well-defined family context. This approach promotes shared principles that educate all members on how to ethically handle estate matters.

Understanding ethics within a family introduces a framework where moral values, transparency, and fairness are prioritized. Families often share core values that serve as the foundation for making equitable decisions. These include honesty, respect, and mutual understanding. By defining these ethics early on, families can develop a unified approach to address estate distribution, which helps avoid conflicts arising from misunderstandings or perceived favoritism. Educating family members on these principles ensures that everyone is aware of what is expected and why certain decisions are made.

Charitable giving presents another dimension of ethical estate planning. Integrating philanthropy into estate distribution can create opportunities for family unity around shared causes, reinforcing a collective sense of purpose. Families can establish charitable trusts or foundations that reflect their values and priorities, allowing them to contribute to societal good while preserving a legacy of generosity. For example, if a family values education, they might set up scholarships benefiting students who lack financial resources. This act not only honors the family's philanthropic goals but also fosters a sense of responsibility and pride among its members.

Guideline: To effectively integrate charitable giving, families should identify causes that align with their shared values and decide how much of the estate will be allocated. This may involve setting up dedicated funds or trusts to manage the contributions systematically.

Ethics in asset management is critical for the sustainable preservation and growth of inherited wealth. Responsible stewardship involves prudent investment, mindful spending, and planning for future generations. Ethical asset management discourages misuse or frivolous spending, emphasizing the importance of maintaining and possibly growing the estate to benefit not just immediate heirs but also future descendants. For instance, establishing clear guidelines for how inherited assets should be managed—such as specifying the types of investments to pursue or outlining permissible uses of funds—can help beneficiaries make wise decisions.

Guideline: Constructing a comprehensive asset management plan is essential. This plan should outline permissible investment strategies, use of assets, and criteria for monetary distribution. Regularly reviewing and updating this plan helps adapt to changing circumstances while adhering to ethical standards.

Regular family meetings play a crucial role in sustaining alignment with established ethical principles and adapting to evolving family dynamics. These gatherings provide a forum for open communication, enabling family members to voice concerns, ask questions, and stay informed about any changes in the estate plan. Consistent dialogue helps ensure that everyone remains on the same page, reducing the likelihood of disputes. Furthermore, these meetings allow the family to revisit and refine ethical guidelines as needed, taking into account new developments such as marriages, births, deaths, or significant acquisitions.

Guideline: Schedule regular family meetings to discuss and review estate plans. These meetings should be structured yet flexible, encouraging participation and feedback from all members. Documentation of discussions and decisions made during these meetings ensures accountability and provides a reference for future deliberations.

By adhering to these ethical principles, families can navigate the complexities of estate distribution thoughtfully and harmoniously. Defining a shared ethical framework, incorporating charitable giving, responsibly managing assets, and maintaining open lines of communication through regular meetings collectively contribute to the equitable and ethical handling of an estate. These practices honor the family's values and traditions, promote unity, and safeguard the interests of both current and future generations.

Forming a Fair Distribution Plan

Developing an equitable estate distribution plan involves navigating the complexities of family dynamics while adhering to ethical obligations. This process, when approached thoughtfully, ensures transparency and understanding among beneficiaries, promotes financial stability, inclusivity, and adaptability over time.

Setting up clear criteria for distribution is paramount to achieving fairness and reducing misunderstandings. Criteria could include asset valuation, specific needs of beneficiaries, or even contribution levels to the family business or caregiving efforts. By establishing these guidelines from the beginning, you create a framework that can be consistently referred to when questions arise. This transparency helps beneficiaries understand the rationale behind your decisions, fostering a sense of trust and reducing potential conflicts.

Involving financial advisors in this process is another critical step. Financial advisors can provide an objective perspective, helping to create a financially stable and sustainable distribution plan. They bring expertise in tax implications, investment strategies, and long-term financial planning, resources that are invaluable in ensuring your estate is managed effectively. Their professional input helps align the estate plan with existing financial circumstances, making sure it remains beneficial and viable over time. For instance, they can advise on setting up trusts to manage assets for minor children or special needs beneficiaries, ensuring their long-term financial security.

Involving family members in the planning process can promote inclusivity and reduce future disputes. Openly discussing your plans with family members allows you to address any concerns or preferences early on. It also provides an opportunity to explain your decisions directly, which can help prevent feelings of favoritism or neglect. This collaborative approach fosters a sense of ownership and respect among family members, as they feel their voices have been heard and considered.

Regularly reviewing and adjusting your estate plan ensures it remains fair and relevant over time. Life is dynamic, and changes such as births, deaths, marriages, divorces, or significant alterations in financial status can impact the fairness and effectiveness of your original distribution plan. Periodic reviews allow you to adapt your plan to reflect these changes, ensuring it remains aligned with your wishes and the evolving needs of your family. This practice not only keeps the plan up-to-date but also reinforces your commitment to fairness and consideration of all involved.

Balancing family dynamics and ethical obligations in estate distribution is essential to avoid conflict and preserve relationships while fulfilling personal wishes. Open communication, reinforced by clear documentation, helps create transparency and understanding among family members. Regular updates and the involvement of legal professionals ensure that the estate plan remains comprehensive and up-to-date. By integrating individual needs and family values into the planning process, you promote a sense of fairness and unity.

Addressing potential conflicts through mediation and fostering an environment of respect and empathy further contributes to harmonious estate distribution. Ethical considerations guide decisions, honoring family traditions and promoting responsible asset management. By taking a thoughtful and inclusive approach, you can create an estate plan that reflects your wishes and supports your family's long-term well-being.

CONCLUSION

As you reach the end of this book, it's time to focus on the key message: empowerment through knowledge. Estate planning may seem daunting, filled with complex legal terms and intricate financial options, but by arming yourself with understanding, you lay a strong foundation for informed decision-making. When you have the right information at your fingertips, you're no longer at the mercy of uncertainty. Instead, you become the master of your own legacy, capable of transforming your intentions into tangible impacts that will benefit future generations.

Reflect for a moment on the insights you've gained here. Think about how each chapter has provided you with not only theoretical knowledge but also actionable strategies. An empowered individual is one who holds the key to their own legacy. This empowerment comes from knowing the principles discussed throughout this book and applying them to your unique circumstances. As you move forward, remember that every step you take in estate planning is a step towards securing peace of mind and stability for your loved ones.

The tools and templates included in this book are designed to facilitate your estate planning journey. These resources are more than just static documents; they are dynamic instruments that can help you streamline the process and make well-informed choices. Utilize these templates as your roadmap, guiding you through the often-turbulent waters of estate planning with clarity and assurance. By filling out these forms and following the guidelines, you create a structured approach that simplifies what once seemed overwhelming.

Throughout our discussion, we've emphasized the importance of practicality. The tools provided are not mere additions but essential components of your estate planning toolkit. They enable you to organize your thoughts, clarify your objectives, and implement your plans efficiently. By using them, you foster confidence in your ability to manage your affairs. Remember, these tools are there to support you, providing a clear path through the complexities of estate management.

As life progresses, so too do your needs and circumstances. Marriage, divorce, the birth of children, or the acquisition of new assets—all these events necessitate a review and potential revision of your estate plans. This book has underscored the dynamic nature of estate planning. It's not a one-time task but an ongoing process that evolves with you. Just as your life story grows and changes, so too should your estate plan. Keeping it up-to-date ensures it remains relevant and effective, meeting your current realities while preserving your legacy.

Consider estate planning as a living document that reflects your life's journey. Regularly reviewing and adapting your plan enables it to serve its purpose effectively. It offers a proactive way to address changes head-on, ensuring your intentions are always accurately represented. This adaptability isn't just practical; it's a reflection of your commitment to those you care about. By allowing your estate plan to evolve, you demonstrate foresight and responsibility, safeguarding the interests of those who matter most to you.

Open communication with family members is paramount. Discussing your estate plans openly helps to mitigate misunderstandings and reduce potential conflicts. Imagine sitting down with your loved ones and saying, "I want to ensure we're all on the same page, so let's discuss my plans openly and honestly." This simple act can pave the way for harmony and understanding. It allows for transparency and fosters trust among your heirs. By addressing concerns and clarifying intentions now, you prevent confusion and disagreements in the future.

Clear, open dialogues about estate planning can strengthen familial bonds. They provide opportunities for sharing values, discussing expectations, and alleviating anxieties. When everyone understands the rationale behind your decisions, they're more likely to respect and honor them. Encouraging these conversations shows that you value your family's input and are committed to maintaining unity. It transforms estate planning from a solitary endeavor into a collaborative effort that benefits everyone involved.

Finally, recognize the long-term impact of your estate planning efforts. Effective planning goes beyond merely distributing assets; it's about creating a lasting legacy. Focus on what you leave behind in terms of values, lessons, and love. Your estate plan is not just a plan for assets; it's a blueprint for the traditions and values you wish to pass on, leaving an enduring mark on your family for years to come. The financial provisions you make are crucial, but so too is the wisdom and guidance you offer.

Think about the stories your family will tell about you, the lessons they'll remember, and the values they'll carry forward. Your estate plan is a testament to your life's work and values. It's an opportunity to teach future generations about stewardship, generosity, and integrity. By carefully considering your legacy, you ensure that your influence extends far beyond your lifetime, shaping the character and aspirations of those who follow.

In conclusion, estate planning is a powerful tool for securing your legacy. By empowering yourself with knowledge, utilizing practical tools, adapting to changing circumstances, fostering open communication, and focusing on long-term impacts, you create a robust and meaningful estate plan. Take control of your estate planning journey today, and know that the steps you take now will resonate positively for generations to come. With the principles and strategies outlined in this book, you are well-equipped to create a lasting legacy—one that reflects your values, supports your loved ones, and stands the test of time.

BONUS SECTION

Table 1: Asset Inventory

Category	Details	Notes/Valuation
Bank Accounts	Bank name, account type, account number	
Investments	Investment type, institution, account number, balance	
Real Estate Properties	Address, mortgage details, estimated value	
Valuables	Description, estimated value	Insured?
Insurance Policies	Insurance type, company, policy number, beneficiaries	
Other Assets	Description (e.g., business stakes, patents)	

Table 2: Important Documents

Document Type	Details	Storage Location
Civil Certificates	Birth, marriage, divorce, death	
Property Documents	Property deed, vehicle title	
Wills and Trusts	Copies of will, trust details	
Financial Documents	Tax returns, loan documentation	
Legal Documents	Power of attorney, guardianship/custody documents	
Contact Information	Lawyers, financial advisors, etc.	

Simple Will Template

WILL of [Full Name]

Article I: Declaration

I, [Full Name], residing at [Full Address], born on [Date of Birth], hereby declare this document to be my Will, prepared while I am of sound mind and not under duress.

Article II: Revocation of Previous Wills

By this document, I revoke all wills and codicils previously made by me.

Article III: Disposition of Property

1. To [Beneficiary Name 1], my [Relationship], I leave [Description of Asset, such as "my house located at" or "my bank account number"].

2. To [Beneficiary Name 2], my [Relationship], I leave [Description of Asset].

Article IV: Appointment of Executor

I appoint [Executor's Name], residing at [Executor's Address], as executor of this will. If [Executor's Name] should decline or be unable to serve as executor, I appoint [Alternate Executor's Name] as substitute executor.

Article V: Final Arrangements

I wish for my burial to be handled according to [Describe your arrangements, e.g., "my prepaid directions with XYZ Funeral Home"].

Signed this [Day] Day of [Month, Year].

_____

[Signature of Testator]

Signed, published, and declared by [Full Name] as his/her Will in our presence, who in his/her presence and in the presence of each other, have hereunto subscribed our names.

_____

[Signature of Witness 1], [Full Address]

_____

[Signature of Witness 2], [Full Address]

Will Template for Parents with Minor Children

WILL of [Full Name]

Article I: Declaration

I, [Full Name], residing at [Full Address], born on [Date of Birth], hereby declare this document to be my Will, prepared while I am of sound mind and not under duress.

Article II: Revocation of Previous Wills

By this document, I revoke all wills and codicils previously made by me.

Article III: Disposition of Property and Guardianship of Minors

1. To [Beneficiary Name 1], my [Relationship], I leave [Description of Asset].

2. For the guardianship of my minor children, I appoint [Guardian's Name] as their legal guardian. Should [Guardian's Name] be unable or unwilling to serve, I appoint [Alternate Guardian's Name] as alternate guardian.

Article IV: Appointment of Executor

I appoint [Executor's Name], residing at [Executor's Address], as executor of this will. If [Executor's Name] should decline or be unable to serve as executor, I appoint [Alternate Executor's Name] as substitute executor.

Article V: Final Arrangements

I wish for my burial to be handled according to [Describe your arrangements, e.g., "my prepaid directions with XYZ Funeral Home"].

Signed this [Day] Day of [Month, Year].

_____

[Signature of Testator]

Signed, published, and declared by [Full Name] as his/her Will in our presence, who in his/her presence and in the presence of each other, have hereunto subscribed our names.

_____

[Signature of Witness 1], [Full Address]

_____

[Signature of Witness 2], [Full Address]

Ethical Will Template: Letter to My Loved Ones

Letter to My Loved Ones
[Date]   Dear [Name(s) of Family/Friends],

As I sit down to write this letter, I find myself reflecting on the values and experiences that have shaped my life. This letter isn't a legal document, but rather a personal message from me to you, where I hope to share some of the principles and beliefs that have guided me, along with my hopes for you as you navigate the future.

1. Life Lessons

- [Lesson 1]: [Description of the lesson and how you learned it].

- [Lesson 2]: [Description of the lesson and how it impacted your life].

2. Personal Values

- Integrity: Always be honest and true to yourself, even when it's challenging. Integrity has been my compass, guiding me through life's ups and downs.

- Compassion: Extend kindness and understanding to others. The moments I have felt the most fulfillment was when I helped someone in need.

3. Family Traditions

I hope you will continue the traditions we have started, whether it's our annual family reunion or the simple Sunday dinners. These traditions have not only brought us joy but also kept us connected as a family.

4. Hopes for the Future

- For [Family Member's Name]: [Specific hopes or dreams you have for this individual].

- For [Another Family Member's Name]: [More hopes or dreams].

5. Advice

- On Challenges: Remember that every challenge is an opportunity to learn and grow. Don't shy away from them; face them with courage.

- On Happiness: Find what makes you happy and pursue it with all your heart. Happiness is a journey, not a destination.

6. Thank You

Thank you for the joy, love, and laughter you have brought into my life. Each one of you has made my journey worthwhile.

7. Final Thoughts

I write this letter with a heart full of love and gratitude. While this may not be a document of legal standing, it is a sincere reflection of my wishes and thoughts. Hold onto these words when you face life's crossroads or during moments of celebration.

With all my love,   [Your Name]

Digital Estate Planning Template

Table 1: Inventory of Digital Assets

Category	Asset Details	Username/Email	Password Management	Notes
Social media	Facebook, Twitter, Instagram, etc.	[Username or email]	[Password manager link]	[Any specific notes or instructions]
Email Accounts	Personal and professional email accounts	[Username or email]	[Password manager link]	[Any specific notes or instructions]
Financial Accounts	PayPal, online banking, investment platforms	[Username or email]	[Password manager link]	[Any specific notes or instructions]
Online Retail	Amazon, eBay, etc.	[Username or email]	[Password manager link]	[Any specific notes or instructions]
Cryptocurrencies	Bitcoin, Ethereum, other wallets	[Username or email]	[Password manager link]	[Any specific notes or instructions]
Subscription Services	Streaming services, online journals, etc.	[Username or email]	[Password manager link]	[Any specific notes or instructions]
Cloud Storage	Google Drive, Dropbox, iCloud, etc.	[Username or email]	[Password manager link]	[Any specific notes or instructions]
Creative Assets	Domains, blogs, copyright materials, GitHub, etc.	[Username or email]	[Password manager link]	[Any specific notes or instructions]

Table 2: Digital Management Instructions After Death

Category	Instructions for Closure or Management	Responsible Person	Additional Details
Social media	E.g., Convert Facebook profile to a memorial page, delete Instagram	[Name of responsible person]	[Any extra instructions]
Email Accounts	E.g., Close accounts after saving necessary correspondence	[Name of responsible person]	[Any extra instructions]
Financial Accounts	E.g., Transfer funds, close accounts	[Name of responsible person]	[Any extra instructions]
Online Retail	E.g., Close accounts and cancel any recurring orders	[Name of responsible person]	[Any extra instructions]
Cryptocurrencies	E.g., Transfer assets to designated beneficiary	[Name of responsible person]	[Any extra instructions]
Subscription Services	E.g., Cancel subscriptions, ensure no recurring billing	[Name of responsible person]	[Any extra instructions]
Cloud Storage	E.g., Download important files, distribute or delete contents	[Name of responsible person]	[Any extra instructions]
Creative Assets	E.g., Transfer ownership of domains, manage online portfolios	[Name of responsible person]	[Any extra instructions]

As a thank you for your interest and support, we are excited to offer an exclusive bonus to enhance your reading experience. In addition to the main content, you now have access to a **free downloadable bonus book**. This additional resource is designed to further deepen your understanding and provide even more value to your journey.

Download Your Bonus Book

To claim your free bonus book, simply scan the QR code below with your smartphone or tablet.

The download will start automatically after scanning.

www.ingramcontent.com/pod-product-compliance
Lightning Source LLC
Chambersburg PA
CBHW062216220526
45471CB00009B/3225